55 AND 54 B.C.
CAESAR'S EXPEDITIONS TO BRITAIN

55 AND 54 B.C.
Caesar's Expeditions
to Britain

Gallic War

Book IV, chapters 20-36, and
Book V, chapters 8-23

edited by
D.A.S. JOHN B.A.

Headmaster,
Wheatley Park School

Published by Bristol Classical Press
General Editor: John H. Betts

Cover illustration: Trooper from a gravestone of one C. Marius,
from the Imperial period (Schreiber–Anderson)

First published in 1969 by Faber and Faber Ltd

Reprinted, with permission, in 1987, 1993 by
Bristol Classical Press
an imprint of
Gerald Duckworth & Co. Ltd
The Old Piano Factory
48 Hoxton Square, London N1 6PB

A catalogue record for this book is available
from the British Library

ISBN 0-86292-280-1

Printed in Great Britain by
Booksprint, Bristol

CONTENTS

(5)

ILLUSTRATIONS

FOREWORD

One might well ask why anyone should want to produce yet another edition of *Caesar* at a time when the Classics, in the face of reorganization, has yet again to prove its worth. It is for such a reason that this reader has been compiled. The book is intended to be used as a middle-school reader but its aim is something more than the sheer grind of ploughing through twenty-five chapters of *Caesar* with all the immense dreariness that this usually entails. Eight sections have been inserted as introductions to specific chapters and it is hoped that such digressions will encourage the pupil to delve into background studies which will bring the text to life. Maps have been added to complete the picture. The sections and notes, it is hoped, will make the pupils familiar with sites and monuments of Roman Britain and consequently the teacher will be able to pursue another study side by side with the reading of the text —a series of projects produced by the pupils. This will widen the pupils' knowledge of Roman Britain, teach them to work independently and provide expeditions of great interest.

The text used throughout is that of the Loeb edition edited by H. J. Edwards. The editor would like to acknowledge his debt to Collingwood and Myres, *Roman Britain and the English Settlements*; Professor Richmond, *Roman Britain*; R. W. Moore, *The Romans in Britain;* M. Wheeler, *Pre-Historic and Roman Wales*; Professor Frère, *Britannia*; and to his third year Classical Sixth pupils who gave unstinted help with the vocabulary.

D. A. S. J.

December 1967

FOREWORD TO 1987 EDITION

The introduction of the new examination at 16+ (the General Certificate of Secondary Education) means that classical texts will now have to be more closely allied to the new criteria. It must be apparent that this edition, first published in 1969, will be totally in line with current thinking and should act as a stimulus to students of the Classics.

July 1987   *D.A.S.J.*

. . . tamen in Britanniam proficisci contendit. . . . (Bk. IV. 20. 3.)

If one studies the history, language, literature of any nation of Southern or Western Europe, one finds that the Romans were the first to leave their mark there. The Roman empire was the instrument by which two forces, Greek civilization and Christianity, were distributed over the world. The Greek contribution was vast and included science, philosophy, music, mathematics, medicine and, above all, literature. Yet the Greeks, for all their artistic achievements, did not have the solidarity and genius for organization which so characterized the Romans.

The history of the Romans begins really with the history of Rome. The earliest contribution was a monarchy and Rome was governed by seven successive kings. Monarchy came to a bitter end in 509 B.C. by a bloodless revolution, but it was a long time before Rome secured a position in Italy itself. She entered into successive wars with Italian tribes and, after many years of success and disappointment, Rome eventually wore her enemies out and by the middle of the third century B.C. Rome was supreme in Italy and ready to embark on a much larger expansion.

Rome's position as mistress of a united Italy after 272 B.C. made her a commercial rival to Carthage and, because of the geography of Italy, her outlook was to the west. During the earlier history, the Greeks were Carthage's natural rivals, and it was in order to cut off the Greeks from the western Mediterranean that Carthage had obtained territory in Sicily and Sardinia. However, Rome's first province was the island of Sicily which she acquired during the First Punic War, but the provincial cities of Sicily paid tribute to Rome and kept independence.

Next, Sardinia and Corsica were gained in 238 B.C. Rome had also secured a hold on the valley of the Po and for the first time we see the might of Rome extending to the natural boundaries of Italy. Military considerations prompted the invasion of Spain in 197 B.C. and the two provinces into which it was formed, Hither and Further Spain, proved to be a liability rather than an asset. After this came the wars against Macedonia and these led to annexation in 148, and in 146 a final settlement was devised for Greece whereby the governor of Macedon had power to interfere when necessary, and Corinth was razed to the ground and its population sold to slavery. Conquest moved apace and in 146 Africa, upon the destruction of Carthage, was secured as a province. An important addition was that of Gallia Transalpina in 130 because Rome wanted to control the Rhône, in view of its strategic importance.

In just over a century, Rome had acquired an unchallenged position throughout the Mediterranean basin. But dark clouds were gathering rapidly. The strain of continuing warfare for a hundred years and a rapid rise to grandeur were to exact their penalty. There was growing up in Rome a sense of individualism. Gone were the values of the community, and increase of power was bringing with it all the attendant evils. Now it was personal ambition and greed that were uppermost in the minds of those in authority. Family life and agricultural prosperity disappeared and into Rome came an influx of unemployed. Here they could not be absorbed into industrial employment which was almost entirely in the hands of slaves, and these unemployed were to form that idle proletariat which was to be the source of trouble in the next century. Tiberius Gracchus, the first Roman reformer, tried to alter this but he lacked diplomacy and experience, and his attempts were doomed to failure. The effort was resumed by his brother Caius Gracchus, a man of greater resources, but he too met the same cruel end as his brother.

The year 70 B.C. saw the consulship of Pompey and Crassus.

Pompey was to be one of the two great military leaders who were to contest the Civil War of 49 B.C. to 44 B.C. Crassus was to be the capitalist: he loved power for its own sake, he was perhaps the type of politician pure and simple who loved the game for itself and was content to bestow rewards and be looked up to as 'boss'. The third member of the First Triumvirate of 60 B.C. was Julius Caesar. These three men pledged to support one another and, with the help of his two allies, Caesar managed to secure for himself the government of the whole of Gaul. In his first four campaigns he repulsed the Helvetii from Switzerland, German tribes under Ariovistus, and conquered the Belgae in the north-east and the Veneti in Brittany. It was while he was so engaged in Gaul that Britain attracted his attention. He was aware that Britain was having a decisive influence on Gallic affairs, and military considerations and economic gain prompted an invasion. Caesar had subdued the warlike tribes in the Low Countries and North-East France and he foresaw that the very existence of a large island within sight and easy access of their shores, populated by Celts of their own race and language, could only be a motive for disaffection. Caesar's invasion of 55 B.C. (as recounted in Book IV, chapters 20–36) was probably nothing more than a demonstration or a punitive expedition. It certainly had a limited objective—Caesar did not aim to conquer the country.

Gaul and Britain were to become Roman provinces. What did this mean in terms of dependence or independence? By the end of the Republic—an approximate date could be reckoned from Caesar's invasions down to 27 B.C.—the word 'provincia' was primarily associated with overseas areas for administration, for which the government in Rome had made itself responsible. The governors were to be regarded as generals whose duty it was to keep law and order. By the time of Caesar, provinces were governed by consuls or praetors after their year of office in Rome.

When the governor arrived at his province, as the representative of the Roman state, his authority could not be questioned. However, each governor had to conduct himself with considerable decorum—although, of course, there are examples of unscrupulous officials—because, if bad reports reached Rome, then he could be deprived of his office and replaced as soon as possible by one of his successors. The governor was emphatically subject to a certain amount of control from the Senate. The provincials were allowed to appeal to Rome and this was done on many an occasion. The authorities in Rome were not blind to the dangers of provincial misgovernment and they were most concerned to protect their provincials. Throughout this period of Caesar's commentaries, every provincial governor was in command of troops, and with these he was expected to maintain law and order.

The governor's only regular assistant was a quaestor who was really his receiver of revenue. The governor usually took along with him his three 'legati'—Caesar had ten in Gaul. These 'legati' could be employed either in a military or judicial sphere. There was also a number of semi-officials who were called 'cohors praetoria'.

The success or failure of provincial administration depended in the main on the quality of the governor. The provincials were allowed to lead the type of life to which they had been accustomed and to manage their own internal affairs. Much depended on the choice of the central government in Rome.

1. *exigua parte . . . reliqua:* tr. 'only a small part of the summer was left'.
3. *proficisci contendit:* 'was set on starting' or 'decided to set out for'.
6. *magno sibi usui fore:* 'it would be very advantageous to him'. There are certain nouns which, when used with the verb 'sum', are put in the dative case, 'usui' being one such example. These nouns are usually in the singular, and such constructions are called predicative datives.
8. *quae:* this is called a connecting relative because it comes at the beginning of a sentence or clause and links up with the sense of the previous clause. Tr. 'all *these*. . . .'
9. *temere:* 'without good reason'.
10. *quisquam:* a pronoun meaning 'anyone' used after a negative particle, e.g. *Haec aio nec quisquam respondet*—'this I say, and no one replies'.
   eis ipsis: i.e. mercatoribus.
12. *Gallias:* the plural form is here used because the Romans regarded Gaul as divided into three distinct areas.
13. *neque quanta:* all the following verbs are in the subjunctive because they are in indirect questions dependent on 'reperire poterat'.

(14)

Book IV, Chapters 20-22
Although the time of the year was unsuitable for an invasion, Caesar decided to put his plans into action because he was convinced that the Gauls were receiving help from this unexplored land. He sent Volusenus in advance while he began to form a camp on the seacoast. Meanwhile ambassadors came to him from Britain and also an embassy from the Morini, a Gallic tribe.

Chapter 20

Exigua parte aestatis reliqua Caesar, etsi in his locis, quod omnis Gallia ad septentriones vergit, maturae sunt hiemes, tamen in Britanniam proficisci contendit, quod omnibus fere Gallicis bellis hostibus nostris inde sumministrata auxilia intellegebat et, si tempus anni ad 5 bellum gerendum deficeret, tamen magno sibi usui fore arbitrabatur, si modo insulam adisset et genus hominum perspexisset, loca, portus, aditus cognovisset; quae omnia fere Gallis erant incognita. Neque enim temere praeter mercatores illo adit quisquam, neque eis ipsis 10 quidquam praeter oram maritimam atque eas regiones quae sunt contra Gallias notum est. Itaque vocatis ad se undique mercatoribus neque quanta esset insulae magnitudo, neque quae aut quantae nationes incolerent, neque quem usum belli haberent aut quibus insti- 15 tutis uterentur, neque qui essent ad maiorum navium multitudinem idonei portus, reperire poterat.

1. *ad haec cognoscenda:* 'cognoscenda' is a gerundive and here it is used like a purpose clause. Tr. 'to gain this knowledge'.

3. *huic mandat:* 'mando' is here followed by an indirect command. Tr. 'he instructed this man to . . .'.

5. *Morinos:* Caesar has mentioned these at the end of Book III of his Gallic Wars. At the end of the summer of 56 B.C. he had advanced against the Morini and Menapii, Belgic tribes in the North—West of Gaul, probably in the vicinity of Calais and Boulogne: hence—'inde erat brevissimus in Britanniam traiectus'. These tribes had attacked his camp from their hiding-places in the forest but, although Caesar repulsed them, he was not able to complete the victory.

7. *superiore aestate:* all this campaign of 56 B.C. against the Veneti is recounted in Book III.

8. *classem:* this is the antecedent of 'quam' and must be translated first.

11. *qui polliceantur:* this is a final relative clause. Tr. 'to promise'.
    dare . . . obtemperare: a slightly unusual construction because verbs of promising in Latin are generally followed by accusative and future infinitive.

13. *pollicitus hortatusque:* take care in your translation of past participles. Tr. 'made a generous promise and encouraged . . .'.

15. *regem:* it was quite a common feature of Roman provincial administration in the days of the Empire to appoint 'client kings' or 'client princes'. Accordingly, Rome was brought into friendly relations with many smaller states whose independence could have easily been threatened by an overpowering neighbour. As a result, Rome became known as the champion of the smaller nations.
    A tribe of Atrebates inhabited Berkshire and it was assumed that Commius would have influence on both sides of the Channel.

18. *magni habebatur:* 'magni' is a genitive of value. Tr. 'his influence was considered to be great'.
    imperat . . . adeat: notice the omission of the 'ut'.

20. *venturum:* 'esse' is regularly omitted with the future infinitive.

21. *omnibus regionibus:* it is probable that Volusenus only explored a small portion of the Kent coast because he was only absent for four days.

24. *renuntiat:* note the use of the present tenses. This is a regular feature in Latin literature and in cases like this they are called historic presents, specially used to add vividness to the description.

Chapter 21

Ad haec cognoscenda, priusquam periclum faceret, idoneum esse arbitratus Gaium Volusenum cum navi longa praemittit. Huic mandat ut exploratis omnibus rebus ad se quam primum revertatur. Ipse cum omnibus copiis in Morinos proficiscitur, quod inde erat 5 brevissimus in Britanniam traiectus. Huc naves undique ex finitimis regionibus et quam superiore aestate ad Veneticum bellum effecerat classem iubet convenire. Interim consilio eius cognito et per mercatores perlato ad Britannos a compluribus insulae civitatibus ad eum 10 legati veniunt qui polliceantur obsides dare atque imperio populi Romani obtemperare. Quibus auditis liberaliter pollicitus hortatusque, ut in ea sententia permanerent, eos domum remittit et cum eis una Commium, quem ipse Atrebatibus superatis regem ibi con- 15 stituerat, cuius et virtutem et consilium probabat et quem sibi fidelem esse arbitrabatur cuiusque auctoritas in his regionibus magni habebatur, mittit. Huic imperat, quas possit, adeat civitates horteturque ut populi Romani fidem sequantur, seque celeriter eo venturum 20 nuntiet. Volusenus perspectis regionibus omnibus, quantum ei facultatis dari potuit qui navi egredi ac se barbaris committere non auderet, quinto die ad Caesarem revertitur quaeque ibi perspexisset renuntiat.

1. *dum:* 'dum' ('while') is regularly used with the present indicative to denote a period of time in the course of which something else happens.
3. *excusarent:* note the final 'qui'.
4. *quod . . . fecissent:* there are two ways of explaining this subjunctive. It could be causal but more probably it is due to the virtual oratio obliqua sense.
9. *tantularum rerum:* a difficult phrase. Tr. 'such trivialities'.
10. *Britanniae anteponendas:* Tr. 'should take precedence over Britain'.
13. *coactis contractisque:* 'raised and concentrated in one spot'.
14. *quod . . . navium longarum:* 'navium' is partitive genitive after 'quod' and the whole phrase is dependent on 'distribuit'. Tr. 'he allotted all the warships he had'.
15. *quaestori:* the quaestors were mainly financial officers. In Caesar's army, their duties, though primarily financial, were not exclusively so. As a provincial quaestor, a young man would gain experience in the field. He could command troops or administer justice.
   legatis: see Historical Background, page 13.
   praefectisque: these were the chief officers of the cavalry and auxiliary infantry. They could well be the leaders of the nations providing the forces. Here it probably refers to the 'praefecti fabrum'—the chief officer of the engineers.
18. *in eundem portum:* although no specific name is given, it seems very probable that this harbour was Boulogne (Portus Itius) which was the regular Roman base in this area during the Empire for crossing to Britain.

Chapter 22

Dum in his locis Caesar navium parandarum causa moratur, ex magna parte Morinorum ad eum legati veniunt, qui se de superioris temporis consilio excusarent, quod homines barbari et nostrae consuetudinis imperiti bellum populo Romano fecissent, seque ea quae 5 imperasset facturos pollicerentur. Hoc sibi Caesar satis opportune accidisse arbitratus, quod neque post tergum hostem relinquere volebat neque belli gerendi propter anni tempus facultatem habebat neque has tantularum rerum occupationes Britanniae anteponendas iudicabat, 10 magnum eis numerum obsidum imperat. Quibus adductis eos in fidem recepit. Navibus circiter LXXX onerariis coactis contractisque quot satis esse ad duas transportandas legiones existimabat, quod praeterea navium longarum habebat quaestori, legatis praefec- 15 tisque distribuit. Huc accedebant XVIII onerariae naves, quae ex eo loco ab milibus passuum octo vento tenebantur quo minus in eundem portum venire possent: has equitibus distribuit. Reliquum exercitum Quinto Titurio Sabino et Lucio Aurunculeio Cottae 20 legatis in Menapios atque in eos pagos Morinorum ab quibus ad eum legati non venerant ducendum dedit; Publium Sulpicium Rufum legatum cum eo praesidio, quod satis esse arbitrabatur, portum tenere iussit.

Chapters 23–30
Caesar crossed to Britain and sailed up the Channel to Deal. The Britons resisted bravely and prompted Caesar to try and attack them on the flank. There was a strong fight on shore and the Romans won the day.

2. *tertia fere vigilia:* abl. of time. The Romans divided the period from sunset to sunrise into four watches, the length of the watch varying according to the time of the year. The third watch began at midnight.

3. *ulteriorem portum:* this is probably Ambleteuse which is north-east of Boulogne.

5. *hora quarta:* the day from sunrise to sunset was divided into twelve hours, these hours varying in length according to the time of the year. As this was August, the time here would be somewhere between 9 and 10 a.m.

6. *in omnibus collibus:* these would be the famous 'white cliffs of Dover'.

8. *montibus angustis:* 'angustis' is a very difficult epithet to explain. It probably means here nothing more than 'steep'.

11. *dum:* unlike the 'dum' of the previous chapter, here 'dum' takes the subjunctive and means 'till'.

12. *ad horam nonam:* i.e. 3 p.m.

13. *tribunis militum:* in the Republican army they were senior officers, six to a legion. Their importance declined with the rise of the legati and soon they became commanders of small contingents or even of ships.

14. *cognosset:* for 'cognovisset'—these shortened forms of the pluperfect subjunctive are quite common.
    monuitque: this is a difficult sentence and the different usages of 'ut' require explanation. The first and second 'ut' mean 'as'. The third 'ut' is used like 'quippe' meaning 'seeing that', while the subjunctive 'administrarentur' is an indirect command dependent on 'monuit'.

15. *rei militaris ratio:* 'tactics'.
    maritimae res: 'navigation'.

17. *ad nutum:* 'at a nod' implying the quiek execution of his orders. Perhaps today we might translate 'wink'.

19. *sublatis:* note the principal parts of this verb.

21. *aperto ac plano litore:* where in fact did Caesar land? It is probable that the favourable wind was a south-westerly which carried him eastwards up Channel to a point somewhere near Deal and Walmer where the shoreland certainly fits in with the description here mentioned.

The Britons sued for peace and promised hostages. Unfortunately for Caesar, the ships carrying the cavalry were caught up in a violent storm. Furthermore, there was a full moon which caused excessively high tides. Caesar's fleet suffered much damage. All this roused the Britons to renewed hostilities.

Chapter 23

His constitutis rebus nactus idoneam ad navigandum tempestatem tertia fere vigilia solvit equitesque in ulteriorem portum progredi et naves conscendere et se sequi iussit. A quibus cum paulo tardius esset administratum, ipse hora circiter diei quarta cum primis navi- 5 bus Britanniam attigit atque ibi in omnibus collibus expositas hostium copias armatas conspexit. Cuius loci haec erat natura, atque ita montibus angustis mare continebatur, uti ex locis superioribus in litus telum adigi posset. Hunc ad egrediendum nequaquam ido- 10 neum locum arbitratus, dum reliquae naves eo convenirent, ad horam nonam in ancoris exspectavit. Interim legatis tribunisque militum convocatis et quae ex Voluseno cognosset et quae fieri vellet ostendit; monuitque, ut rei militaris ratio, maxime ut maritimae res 15 postularent, ut quae celerem atque instabilem motum haberent, ad nutum et ad tempus omnes res ab eis administrarentur. His dimissis et ventum et aestum uno tempore nactus secundum dato signo et sublatis ancoris circiter milia passuum septem ab eo loco progressus 20 aperto ac plano litore naves constituit.

1. *barbari:* it is worth noting that the Romans applied this
   epithet 'barbarian' to anyone other than a Roman or Greek.
   praemisso: the force of the compound verb gives the meaning
   'sent *forward*'.
2. *essedariis:* at this time the Britons, unlike the Gauls of this
   period, used chariots in warfare. In many ways they were
   a sort of cavalry or mounted infantry. Some writers believe
   that these chariots were armed with scythes just like those
   described by Xenophon, a Greek historian, in his account
   of the March of the Ten Thousand. However, Caesar does
   not mention this, and the silence of the best authorities lends
   weight to Caesar's simple description.
3. *consuerunt:* contracted form of 'consueverunt'.
4. *egredi:* 'prohibeo' when it means 'to prevent' is regularly followed by the infinitive in Caesar.
5. *in alto:* 'in deep water'. 'Altum' is regularly used in the poets,
   particularly Virgil, to mean 'the deep'.
6. *militibus:* this is in the dative case after the gerundive 'desiliendum'. Tr. 'the troops had to jump down'.
   ignotis locis, impeditis manibus: abl. abs.
9. *cum:* 'while'.
11. *membris expeditis:* 'with all their limbs free'. In military langu-
    age, a 'miles expeditus' means a 'light-armed soldier' or
    'swiftly marching soldier'.
13. *perterriti:* the force of the 'per' means '*very* frightened'.
    generis: this is genitive case after 'imperitus'. Tr. 'with no
    experience in this type of fighting'.
14. *eadem . . . quo:* Tr. 'did not press on with the same eagerness
    and zeal as . . .'

4. *ad latus apertum:* Tr. 'the exposed flank'.
5. *fundis:* the archers were obviously Cretan and the slingers
   Balearic—both forming part of the auxilia. See page 44.
   The 'tormenta' were probably the catapulta which would
   carry an arrow for 400 yards, a cross-bow mounted on a
   frame, and the 'ballista' rather like a catapulta but heavier
   and designed for throwing stones. It had a range of 300
   yards.
6. *usui:* see note on chapter 20. Tr. 'this proved very useful to
   our men'.

(22)

Chapter 24

At barbari, consilio Romanorum cognito praemisso
equitatu et essedariis, quo plerumque genere in proeliis
uti consuerunt, reliquis copiis subsecuti nostros navibus
egredi prohibebant. Erat ob has causas summa difficultas, quod naves propter magnitudinem nisi in alto 5
constitui non poterant, militibus autem ignotis locis,
impeditis manibus, magno et gravi onere armorum
oppressis, simul et de navibus desiliendum et in fluctibus
consistendum et cum hostibus erat pugnandum, cum
illi aut ex arido aut paulum in aquam progressi omnibus 10
membris expeditis, notissimis locis audacter tela coni-
cerent et equos insuefactos incitarent. Quibus rebus
nostri perterriti atque huius omnino generis pugnae
imperiti non eadem alacritate ac studio quo in pedestri-
bus uti proeliis consuerant nitebantur.

Chapter 25

Quod ubi Caesar animadvertit, naves longas, quarum
et species erat barbaris inusitatior et motus ad usum
expeditior, paulum removeri ab onerariis navibus et
remis incitari et ad latus apertum hostium constitui
atque inde fundis, sagittis, tormentis hostes propelli ac 5
summoveri iussit; quae res magno usui nostris fuit. Nam
et navium figura et remorum motu et inusitato genere
tormentorum permoti barbari constiterunt ac paulum
modo pedem rettulerunt. Atque nostris militibus cunc-

(23)

10. *qui:* the antecedent must be understood. This is quite regular in the form 'is qui'. Tr. 'the soldier who was . . .'.

decimae legionis: the 10th was Caesar's most trusted legion. In Book I of his Gallic Wars, Caesar said that 'if no one else would follow him, then he would go alone with the 10th legion about which he had no doubts'. It is mentioned on several other occasions in his Commentaries, usually in a favourable light.

13. *aquilam:* see note on page 45.

ego certe: notice the emphatic pronoun here, 'I, at any rate'.

15. *se ex navi proiecit:* notice here the word order. Caesar regularly, when using the reflexive with the verb, makes use of a bracketing word order and places everything, that the verb governs, in between the reflexive pronoun and the verb.

16. *coepit:* this is a perfect stem of the verb 'incipio' which has a regular form 'incepi'. It is always followed by a prolative infinitive.

inter se: 'each other'.

19. *appropinquarunt:* contracted form of 'appropinquaverunt' and this verb is intransitive ('hostibus' is dative).

1. *pugnatum est:* an impersonal use of the verb where stress is put on the action rather than the doer of the action. Tr. 'both sides fought fiercely'.

3. *alius alia ex navi:* Tr. 'any man from any ship'. This is a very condensed phrase which is common in Latin—e.g. *'alius aliud dicit'* = one man says one thing, another man says something else. This is also regularly found in Greek.

10. *scaphas:* this is a little boat or skiff.

speculatoria navigia: these were small fast vessels which were used for scouting, as the word 'speculatoria' implies.

11. *laborantes:* here 'laborare' means 'to be in difficulties'.

12. *simul:* = simul atque.

15. *equites:* the cavalry had not been able to maintain their course because the change of wind forced them back to Ambleteuse. See chapter 23.

17. *Caesari:* dative after 'defuit'. Note that most compounds of 'sum' govern a dative.

tantibus, maxime propter altitudinem maris, qui deci- 10
mae legionis aquilam ferebat, contestatus deos, ut ea
res legioni feliciter eveniret, 'Desilite', inquit, 'milites,
nisi vultis aquilam hostibus prodere: ego certe meum
rei publicae atque imperatori officium praestitero'. Hoc
cum voce magna dixisset, se ex navi proiecit atque in 15
hostes aquilam ferre coepit. Tum nostri cohortati inter
se, ne tantum dedecus admitteretur, universi ex navi
desiluerunt. Hos item ex proximis navibus cum con-
spexissent, subsecuti hostibus appropinquarunt.

Chapter 26

Pugnatum est ab utrisque acriter. Nostri tamen, quod
neque ordines servare neque firmiter insistere neque
signa subsequi poterant, atque alius alia ex navi quibus-
cumque signis occurrerat se adgregabat, magnopere
perturbabantur; hostes vero notis omnibus vadis, ubi ex 5
litore aliquos singulares ex navi egredientes conspex-
rant, incitatis equis impeditos adoriebantur, plures
paucos circumsistebant, alii ab latere aperto in universos
tela coniciebant. Quod cum animadvertisset Caesar,
scaphas longarum navium, item speculatoria navigia 10
militibus compleri iussit et, quos laborantes conspexerat,
his subsidia submittebat. Nostri, simul in arido constiterunt, suis omnibus consecutis in hostes impetum fecerunt
atque eos in fugam dederunt; neque longius prosequi
potuerunt, quod equites cursum tenere atque insulam 15
capere non potuerant. Hoc unum ad pristinam fortu-
nam Caesari defuit.

3. *daturos:* see note on chapter 21, line 20.
5. *supra:* chapter 21.
6. *praemissum:* here 'esse' has been omitted with the perfect infinitive.
   oratoris modo: 'in his capacity of ambassador'.
9. *culpam in multitudinem coniecerunt:* note again the bracketing order as explained with the use of the reflexive in chapter 25.
10. *ignosceretur:* another impersonal use. Tr. 'sought pardon'.
11. *cum:* it is used here with a concessive sense 'although'.
    ultro: literally means 'further', 'beyond', and comes to mean 'of their own accord'.
13. *intulissent:* subjunctive is due to the virtual oratio obliqua, that is, the sentence is part of Caesar's complaint.
    imprudentiae: dative case after the verb 'ignoscere'.
14. *obsidesque imperavit:* the verb 'impero' is usually followed by 'ut' or 'ne' introducing a noun clause—mihi imperavit ut donum irem—he ordered me to go home. It also governs an indirect object 'mihi'. Here the verb has the meaning of 'to levy' and is used in a transitive sense.

1. *post diem quartum quam:* equivalent to 'die quarto postquam'.
2. *est ventum:* impersonal use. Tr. 'the fourth day after the arrival in Britain'.
3. *supra:* chapter 22.
   ex superiore portu: i.e. from Ambleteuse.
8. *ad inferiorem partem insulae:* if the wind changed from southwest to north-east, this is then a probable reference to Cornwall. Cornwall was an area which was known to the Romans at this time because of its export of tin.
9. *sui:* objective genitive, 'to themselves'.

(26)

Chapter 27

Hostes proelio superati, simul atque se ex fuga receperunt, statim ad Caesarem legatos de pace miserunt, obsides daturos quaeque imperasset sese facturos polliciti sunt. Una cum his legatis Commius Atrebas venit, quem supra demonstraveram a Caesare in Britanniam 5 praemissum. Hunc illi e navi egressum, cum ad eos oratoris modo Caesaris mandata deferret, comprehenderant atque in vincula coniecerant: tum proelio facto remiserunt, et in petenda pace eius rei culpam in multitudinem coniecerunt et propter imprudentiam ut ignos- 10 ceretur petiverunt. Caesar questus quod, cum ultro in continentem legatis missis pacem ab se petissent, bellum sine causa intulissent, ignoscere imprudentiae dixit obsidesque imperavit; quorum illi partem statim dederunt, partem ex longinquioribus locis arcessitam paucis 15 diebus sese daturos dixerunt. Interea suos remigrare in agros iusserunt, principesque undique convenire et se civitatesque suas Caesari commendare coeperunt.

Chapter 28

His rebus pace confirmata, post diem quartum quam est in Britanniam ventum, naves XVIII, de quibus supra demonstratum est, quae equites sustulerant, ex superiore portu leni vento solverunt. Quae cum appropinquarent Britanniae et ex castris viderentur, tanta 5 tempestas subito coorta est ut nulla earum cursum tenere posset, sed aliae eodem unde erant profectae referrentur, aliae ad inferiorem partem insulae, quae est propius solis occasum, magno sui cum periculo deicerentur; quae tamen ancoris iactis cum fluctibus 10

11. *adversa nocte:* Tr. 'in a night of bad weather'.
12. *petierunt:* yet another contracted form for 'petiverunt'.

2. *Oceano:* this must be a vague generalization for somewhere off the Kent coast.
3. *id erat incognitum:* Gallic pilots, who had used the Channel considerably before Caesar arrived, must have been aware of this fact. However, these same pilots were certainly not going to give information to someone who was likely to deprive them of their cross-Channel monopoly.
4. *transportandum curaverat:* this is a common construction of 'curare' and the gerundive meaning 'to see to'. E.g. He saw to it that the bridge was built = *pontem aedificandum curavit.*
8. *administrandi:* a genitive of the gerund after 'facultas'.
   auxiliandi: from 'auxilior', not a particularly common verb.
13. *possent:* a consecutive subjunctive. Tr. 'for there were no other ships to carry them back'.
14. *usui:* a predicative dative, see chapter 25.

CAMPS

. . . paucitatem militum ex castrorum exiguitate cognoscerent. . . .
(Bk. IV. 30. 4.)

There were three different types:
   (a) *Temporary camps*
   (b) *Semi-permanent camps*
   (c) *Permanent camps*

(28)

complerentur, necessario adversa nocte in altum pro-
vectae continentem petierunt.

Chapter 29

Eadem nocte accidit ut esset luna plena, qui dies
maritimos aestus maximos in Oceano efficere consuevit,
nostrisque id erat incognitum. Ita uno tempore et
longas naves, quibus Caesar exercitum transportandum
curaverat quasque in aridum subduxerat, aestus com- 5
pleverat et onerarias, quae ad ancoras erant deligatae,
tempestas adflictabat, neque ulla nostris facultas aut
administrandi aut auxiliandi dabatur. Compluribus
navibus fractis reliquae cum essent funibus, ancoris reli-
quisque armamentis amissis ad navigandum inutiles, 10
magna, id quod necesse erat accidere, totius exercitus
perturbatio facta est. Neque enim naves erant aliae
quibus reportari possent, et omnia deerant quae ad
reficiendas naves erant usui, et, quod omnibus con-
stabat hiemari in Gallia oportere, frumentum his in 15
locis in hiemem provisum non erat.

(a) *Temporary camps*
  *These are enclosures of varying size as Roman troops on the
move used to build some sort of fortification round themselves
every night. The tents were pitched in these marching camps and
an 'agger' was built around it and the ditch in front. Because
of their slight character many of these camps disappeared. In
theory, they were laid out to a textbook plan. The whole area
would be in the shape of a rectangle with rounded corners. Four
gates are prescribed. It was divided into the usual three parts*

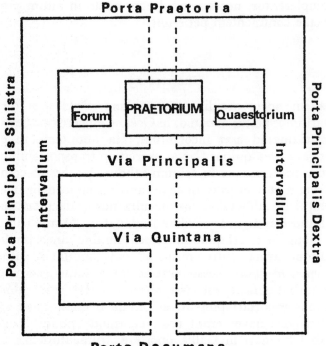

A PLAN OF A ROMAN CAMP

and in the centre was the 'praetorium'. This plan was not exactly followed in Britain. One authority has prescribed 83 acres for an army of 46,000, Professor Richmond estimated that in a British camp there would be eight men to every 10 square feet. For a century, it would be 120 feet by 30 feet. This would mean tents were very closely packed together and the best example in Wales is at Y-Pigwn in Breconshire.

(b) *Semi-permanent camps*
These represent the half-way stage between temporary and

permanent camps and they could be used for a complete campaign.

The works are slightly bigger. The rampart about 20 feet wide would be strengthened by wooden stakes or even a wooded palisade. This type of camp would be equipped with watch-towers and lightly metalled streets. There are very few examples in Britain and in the main they are difficult to distinguish because they have been overlaid by permanent camps.

(c) *Permanent camps*

These were designed to hold auxiliary regiments and were a screen for the legionary fortresses in the background. They have been sited for strategical rather than tactical purposes. They were placed on road junctions or often the site chosen would be a low hill near a stream or river. They are of three sizes:

    (a) *From two to three acres would hold a quingenary cohort (500)*

    (b) *From 4 to 5 acres would hold a milliary cohort (1,000 infantry or 500 cavalry).*

    (c) *From 7 to 8 acres would hold a 'ala miliaria' (1,000 cavalry).*

In Britain, there is only one example of the third class and that is at Corbridge.

3. *Romanis:* dative after 'deesse'.

5. *hoc:* ablative neuter 'owing to the fact that'.
7. *optimum factu:* 'factu' is a supine in -u used with adjectives. It never takes an object. Cf. a favourite phrase in Virgil *'mirabile dictu'*—'wonderful to tell'. Tr. here 'the best thing in the doing' = the best thing to do.
   duxerunt: here 'duco' means 'consider'.
9. *his superatis:* an abl. abs. with a conditional sense 'if these . . .'.
11. *rursus coniuratione facta:* Tr. 'renewed their oaths to stand together'.

2. *ex eventu:* 'from the misfortune'.
   ex eo quod: 'from the fact that'.

(32)

Chapter 30

Quibus rebus cognitis principes Britanniae, qui post
proelium ad Caesarem convenerant, inter se collocuti,
cum equites et naves et frumentum Romanis deesse in-
tellegerent et paucitatem militum ex castrorum exiguitate cognoscerent, quae hoc erant etiam angustiora, 5
quod sine impedimentis Caesar legiones transportaverat,
optimum factu esse duxerunt rebellione facta frumento
commeatuque nostros prohibere et rem in hiemem pro-
ducere, quod his superatis aut reditu interclusis nemi-
nem postea belli inferendi causa in Britanniam transi- 10
turum confidebant. Itaque rursus coniuratione facta
paulatim ex castris discedere ac suos clam ex agris
deducere coeperunt.

Chapters 31-36
Caesar had to make counter preparations, getting in
provisions and trying to repair the damaged fleet. His
Seventh Legion was sent to collect corn and was sur-
prised and surrounded by the Britons whose main
method of attack was from chariots. Caesar hastened to
the relief of his men and the result was an honourable
draw. The Britons then sent envoys to treat for peace.
Caesar decided to double the number of hostages and
then returned to the Continent.

Chapter 31

At Caesar, etsi nondum eorum consilia cognoverat,
tamen et ex eventu navium suarum et ex eo, quod

(33)

3. *fore id quod accidit:* 'id' is subject of 'fore'. Tr. 'he suspected that events would turn out as they did'. 'Accidit' is indicative because it does not represent what Caesar thought.

6. *quae:* the relative pronoun 'qui' agrees in gender and number with a noun in a preceding sentence. The noun to which it refers is called its antecedent, e.g. *Servum misi quem habui.*

   Here Caesar has an inversion of the antecedent and the relative where we would have expected *'earum navium quae'.*

9. *administraretur:* another impersonal use of the verb.

10. *navibus amissis:* the abl. abs. can be translated in various ways there is no one set rule. In chapter 30 it had a conditional sense, here a concessive one.—Tr. 'though twelve ships had been lost'.

1. *frumentatum:* supine in -um to express purpose. This usage of the supine is normally only used to express purpose after verbs of motion.

2. *septima:* we know very little about this legion. In later campaigns to Britain under the emperor Claudius (A.D. 41–54), we know that the force which landed on the coast of Kent in A.D. 43 included four legions, the IInd Augusta, the XXth, the IXth Hispana and the XIVth Gemina.

3. *cum:* 'while'.

4. *ventitaret:* this is a frequentative form of the simple verb 'venio' and means 'kept coming'.

6. *quam consuetudo ferret:* 'greater than usual'.

8. *novi consili:* partitive genitive after 'aliquid'.

12. *paulo longius:* 'some little way'.

14. *conferta legione:* 'the legion was crowded together'.

obsides dare intermiserant, fore id quod accidit suspica-
batur. Itaque ad omnes casus subsidia comparabat.
Nam et frumentum ex agris cotidie in castra conferebat 5
et, quae gravissime adflictae erant naves, earum materia
atque aere ad reliquas reficiendas utebatur et quae ad
eas res erant usui ex continenti comportari iubebat.
Itaque, cum summo studio a militibus administraretur,
XII navibus amissis, reliquis ut navigari commode 10
posset effecit.

Chapter 32

Dum ea geruntur, legione ex consuetudine una frumentatum missa, quae appellabatur septima, neque ulla
ad id tempus belli suspicione interposita, cum pars
hominum in agris remaneret, pars etiam in castra ventitaret, ei qui pro portis castrorum in statione erant 5
Caesari nuntiaverunt pulverem maiorem quam consuetudo ferret in ea parte videri, quam in partem legio
iter fecisset. Caesar id quod erat suspicatus, aliquid novi
a barbaris initum consili, cohortes quae in stationibus
erant secum in eam partem proficisci, ex reliquis duas 10
in stationem cohortes succedere, reliquas armari et confestim sese subsequi iussit. Cum paulo longius a castris
processisset, suos ab hostibus premi atque aegre sustinere et conferta legione ex omnibus partibus tela conici
animadvertit. Nam quod omni ex reliquis partibus 15
demesso frumento pars una erat reliqua, suspicati hostes
huc nostros esse venturos noctu in silvis delituerant; tum
dispersos depositis armis in metendo occupatos subito
adorti paucis interfectis reliquos incertis ordinibus per-
turbaverant, simul equitatu atque essedis circumde- 20
derant.

(35)

2. *perequitant:* this chapter is a vivid account of chariot fighting. Caesar wants to convey this feeling to his reader and throughout the chapter all indicative verbs are in the present tense. These are called historic presents and heighten the dramatic effect.

4. *insinuaverunt:* the use of this verb is very appropriate. It has a 'creepy' sense and Virgil uses it in his description of a snake. Here it means 'to work their way into'.

5. *aurigae:* Tacitus in his 'Agricola' has something to say about the status of drivers and fighters. In his chapter 12 he says 'but certain tribes also fight from chariots: the driver (auriga) has the place of honour, the combatants are mere retainers'. (Loeb).

11. *equos sustinere:* 'keep control of'.

12. *per temonem percurrere:* this was a tactic usually employed by the fighters. They would run along the pole to throw their weapons from closer range and then smartly retreat.

1. *perturbatis nostris:* this could be an abl. abs. as implied by some editors, but a dative case dependent on 'auxilium tulit' is equally attractive.
   novitate pugnae: by its very position this can be considered as an afterthought to explain 'quibus rebus'.
   tempore opportunissimo: abl. of time. Tr. 'in the very nick of time'.

6. *brevi tempore intermisso:* simply 'after a brief interval'.

8. *qui erant . . . reliqui:* these are the people who had not originally supported their leaders but now were conscious of a last-minute stand.

9. *quae . . . continerent:* a subjunctive due to consecutive force. Tr. 'storms severe enough to'.

11. *dimiserunt:* 'dimitto' can mean 'to send in all directions'. Here it is further amplified by 'in omnes partes'.

13. *sui:* this is genitive of 'se'.

14. *daretur:* subjunctive in an indirect question.
   expulissent: pluperfect subjunctive of a conditional clause in indirect speech. It represents a future perfect of direct speech.

(36)

Chapter 33

Genus hoc est ex essedis pugnae. Primo per omnes partes perequitant et tela coniciunt atque ipso terrore equorum et strepitu rotarum ordines plerumque perturbant, et cum se inter equitum turmas insinuaverunt, ex essedis desiliunt et pedibus proeliantur. Aurigae interim paula- 5 tim ex proelio excedunt atque ita currus collocant, ut, si illi a multitudine hostium premantur, expeditum ad suos receptum habeant. Ita mobilitatem equitum, stabilitatem peditum in proeliis praestant, ac tantum usu cotidiano et exercitatione efficiunt uti in declivi ac 10 praecipiti loco incitatos equos sustinere et brevi moderari ac flectere et per temonem percurrere et in iugo insistere et se inde in currus citissime recipere consuerint.

Chapter 34

Quibus rebus perturbatis nostris novitate pugnae tempore opportunissimo Caesar auxilium tulit: namque eius adventu hostes constiterunt, nostri se ex timore receperunt. Quo facto ad lacessendum et ad committendum proelium alienum esse tempus arbitratus suo se 5 loco continuit et brevi tempore intermisso in castra legiones reduxit. Dum haec geruntur, nostris omnibus occupatis qui erant in agris reliqui discesserunt. Secutae sunt continuos complures dies tempestates, quae et nostros in castris continerent et hostem a pugna prohiber- 10 ent. Interim barbari nuntios in omnes partes dimiserunt paucitatemque nostrorum militum suis praedicaverunt et, quanta praedae faciendae atque in perpetuum sui liberandi facultas daretur, si Romanos castris expulissent, demonstraverunt. His rebus celeriter magna multi- 15 tudine peditatus equitatusque coacta ad castra venerunt.

(37)

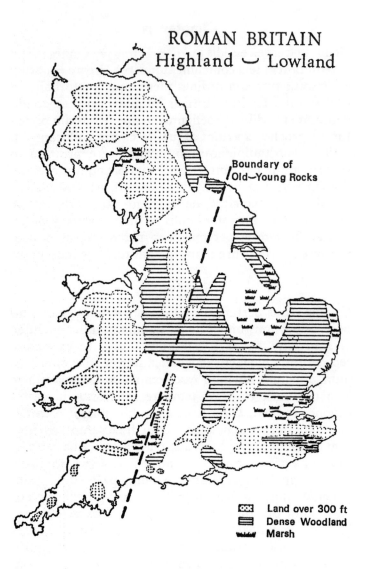

ROMAN BRITAIN
Highland ⌣ Lowland

Boundary of
Old~Young Rocks

Land over 300 ft
Dense Woodland
Marsh

(38)

Villas

. . . deinde omnibus longe lateque aedificiis incensis se in castra receperunt. (Bk. IV. 35. 9.)

During the Iron Age agriculture was perhaps the most prominent feature of the economy of the southern half of Britain. The largest part of the inhabitants were country folk who lived in villages or on isolated farms: these farms were eventually to be called 'villas'. The Belgae appear to have made much of these isolated farms and from these dwellings arose the villa system.

The Severn to the Tees was an imaginary line which separated Highland Britain to the North from Lowland Britain to the South. Nearly all the villas have been discovered to the south and east of that line. This is significant: they represent the good agricultural land of the Roman period. About five hundred villa sites are known, especially in North Kent, the Hampshire Basin and in the Cotswolds and Mendip regions. These represent a most productive area. There are areas which are most conspicuous for their lack of sites, notably the Weald where the forests were unsuitable and the Midlands with its clay lands. Apart from these two main areas there are a number of villa sites in North Lincolnshire and East Yorkshire which became prosperous in the late fourth century. There is even one isolated example in the Pennines and one near Durham. There are, too, a number of examples in Wales although here they are mainly sited along the Vale of Glamorgan, a sheltered spot exposed to the sun and close to water. Essentially, the villa is a south-eastern type of structure. The reason was that villa-owners tended to chose a rather special type of site. It had to be a sheltered scarp of the downlands with plenty of sunshine and sheltered from the wind. The villas of the Cotswolds nestle warmly on the sides of valleys, and Chedworth villa near Cirencester is a supreme example of this.

A Roman villa was not simply luxury, rather it was to be a

profit-making farm and as such it was always associated with agriculture or industry. The owners were by and large native Britons who took on some form of Romanization; occasionally they were retired soldiers or officials and perhaps were immigrants in that sense. Consequently, the move was spontaneous and, unlike urban Romanization, it continued till the end of the Roman period. Most of the Roman villas that have been found were originally Belgic farms and examples have been discovered at Newport on the Isle of Wight, Park Street (St. Albans) and Lockleys, near Welwyn.

The first type of Roman villa was simply a rectangular building consisting of four or five rooms. It was quite a simple construction.

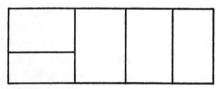

LOCKLEYS

The same story is found at Ditchley in Oxfordshire. There are three main types of villa:

(a) *Barn house.*
(b) *Corridor house.*
(c) *Courtyard house.*

The three types represent the different stages in the evolutionary development of the villa.

(a) *Barn house*

The building was long and oblong and divided into three parts. The aisle was separated from the nave by timber posts and the ends of the house were walled off from the residence. It was a poor type of dwelling, probably belonging to a bailiff. It represents the first stage in the development of the villa.

(40)

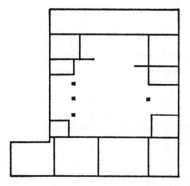

(b) *Corridor house*

Here there is considerable development and this villa repre-sents the next grade in economic prosperity. Where there was one corridor it was called a bi-partite villa but examples of the tripartite villa have been found. Ditchley is a good example of the corridor type. The servants' quarters were at the south end while the owner lived in great splendour. A similar pattern was found at Hambledon in Buckinghamshire.

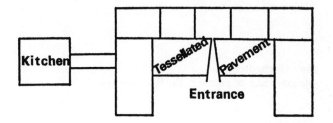

(c) *Courtyard house*

The change from corridor house to a courtyard house repre-sents mainly an increase in the size of the household. The barns were kept separate from the main building. One of the largest

(41)

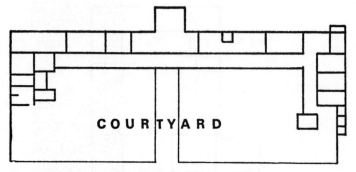

COURTYARD

is at Woodchester in Gloucestershire: others can be seen at Bignor in Sussex and Chedworth. At Northleigh in Oxfordshire there are traces of an earlier building which was in fact a corridor building later developed into a double courtyard structure.

The exterior of the villa had the tiled type of roof with elaborate decorations. Inside, most of the walls were decorated with wall plaster, plain or marbled. The chief glory was perhaps

---

2. *fore:* cf. chapter 31.
   celeritate: abl. of manner. Tr. 'by their speed'.

7. *quos:* connecting relative.
8. *tanto spatio . . . quantum:* Tr. 'the Romans followed after, as far as their speed and strength enabled' (Loeb).
10. *aedificiis:* see introduction to the chapter.

the mosaic pavement. There was the plain type associated with the barn-type villa. Perhaps the most common was the geometric pattern—fine examples of this can be seen at Bignor. The figured pavement was not quite so frequent but a good hunting scene has been unearthed at Coker in Somerset. The scene contains mythological figures and shows the taste of the Romano-British villa owner—he was associated with the myths of ancient Rome.

The villa was clearly equipped with amenities. It had a water supply, drainage and sanitation. Heating varied from the simple hearth to the central heating system called the 'hypocaust'. Cooking was done in a low-domed oven and the fuel used was charcoal and wood. There are few indications as to the type of furnishing used.

It is to be hoped that pupils will visit some of the many fine examples of villas which are to be found in the south-eastern half of the country and see for themselves the scope of villa development.

Chapter 35

Caesar, etsi idem quod superioribus diebus acciderat fore videbat, ut, si essent hostes pulsi, celeritate periculum effugerent, tamen nactus equites circiter XXX, quos Commius Atrebas, de quo ante dictum est, secum transportaverat, legiones in acie pro castris constituit. 5 Commisso proelio diutius nostrorum militum impetum hostes ferre non potuerunt ac terga verterunt. Quos tanto spatio secuti quantum cursu et viribus efficere potuerunt, complures ex eis occiderunt, deinde omnibus longe lateque aedificiis incensis se in castra receperunt. 10

2. *his:* 'for them'.

4. *infirmis navibus:* 'with unseaworthy ships'.
5. *hiemi navigationem . . . existimabat:* lit. 'he did not think that shipping ought to be subjected to the winter'.

THE ROMAN ARMY

. . . Labieno in continente cum tribus legionibus et equitum milibus duobus relicto. . . . (Bk. V. 8. 1.)

From the very earliest times military service was regarded as an essential feature of citizenship whereby people possessing more than a certain amount of property were compelled to serve. This meant that the poorest citizens were exempt from service. This inequality was lessened by certain reforms and eventually property qualification was abolished and any citizen could serve.

The backbone of the Roman army was the legion. The smallest contingent of the legion was the group of eight men who shared a tent. Ten of these groups formed a company called a 'centuria' which was under the command of a centurion. Six centuries formed a cohort and ten cohorts made up a legion. By the time of Augustus, the first cohort (whose leader was called 'primus pilus') contained 1,000 men, whilst the others numbered 500 each, Each cohort was divided into three maniples,

(44)

Chapter 36

Eodem die legati ab hostibuṣ missi ad Caesarem de pace
venerunt. His Caesar numerum obsidum quem ante
imperaverat duplicavit eosque in continentem adduci
iussit, quod propinqua die aequinocti infirmis navibus
hiemi navigationem subiciendam non existimabat. Ipse 5
idoneam tempestatem nactus paulo post mediam noc-
tem naves solvit; quae omnes incolumes ad continentem
pervenerunt, sed ex eis onerariae duae eosdem, quos
reliqui, portus capere non potuerunt et paulo infra
delatae sunt.

l.2.94

---

*each commanded by its senior centurion (thirty maniples). All in
all, the legion totalled about 6,000 men and this included a
squadron of 120 legionary cavalry, probably distributed among
the centuries for administrative purposes.*

*The chief officer was the legionary legate (legatus legionis),
a position reserved for men of senatorial rank. Under him there
were six military tribunes who were usually young men with no
military experience—but it was an office recognized as the
natural step in a senatorial career. This office was largely administrative. Next in line were the sixty centurions whose aim
was to become ultimately a camp-prefect (praefectus castrorum).
This latter officer was virtually the second in command and was
mainly responsible for internal organization and training. Finally, at the bottom end of the scale came the junior officers:*

(a) *Aquilifer—the standard-bearer of the silver eagle which
was mounted on a pole fitted with lateral spikes. The
'aquila' was identified with a spirit of a legion and its
loss was an indelible disgrace.*

(b) *Optio—a sub-centurion.*

(c) *Signifer–another standard-bearer distinguished by
special helmets which were of bear-skin.*

(d) *Tesserarius—a sort of orderly sergeant.*

(e) *Tubicen—a trumpeter who blew on his 'tuba', a long straight trumpet used for controlling tactical movements in the field.*

(f) *Cornicen—similar to the above but instead he blew on a circular trumpet.*

Each legion was distinguished by a number and title. Permanent numbers were first given by Caesar and Pompey, and regularized by Augustus. As well as the number, there were titles— for example, a legion might have a name taken from the province where it had fought in a distinguished manner. A title was found in York bearing the inscription LEG. IX. HISPANA. It might have a title commemorating the emperor by whom the legion was formed—LEG. II. AUGUSTA. The titles could well commemorate the success of a legion in campaign or might indicate the locality where the legion was stationed—LEG. XX. VALERIA VICTRIX DEVENSIS (of Deva—Chester). It was also known for more than one legion to have the same number—the II AUGUSTA and the II ADIUTRIX both served in Britain.

The paraphernalia of a legionary soldier was considerable. There was the hob-nailed boot (caliga), a short leather trousers (bracae), a tunic (tunica), a scarf (focale), a cloak (sagum), a helmet (galea), a belt (cingulum militare), and a long cylindri-

cal shield (*scutum*). *The soldier carried the 'pilum' and on the right-hand side the short-armed 'gladius' which was usually suspended from the baldric (balteus); on the left-hand side he would have the dagger (pugio).*

The pay of a private soldier did vary but under the Republic he would receive 225 denarii in three instalments. The officer's pay was amazingly higher than that of a private and a 'praefectus castrorum' would expect anything up to 15,000 denarii.

In battle, the legion was drawn up in three lines of cohorts, with a gap between each line. The spaces in the front line were covered by the cohorts in the second line:

After the engagement of the first line, the second line would move up to take its place and similarly the third line would relieve the second line. When a legion was not in active service, it had to be subject to training and fatigues. There were the familiar route march and exercises to be done, and road-making, building and quarrying were all part of a soldier's life.

Book V, Chapters 8-11
Caesar left Labienus to watch Gaul and he himself crossed to Britain for a second time. He marched inland for twelve miles and defeated the Britons in his first engagement. While pursuing the enemy, he received news that his fleet had been seriously damaged in a storm. Caesar halted the pursuit, returned to the coast and repaired his losses.

1. *His rebus gestis:* this is a reference to the opening chapters of Book V. Caesar was spending the winter in Cisalpine Gaul (a territory identified today as a part of Northern Italy) and Illyricum (modern Dalmatia and Albania), while a fleet built in his absence had been assembled at Boulogne. Meanwhile he set out for the territory of the Treveri and decided to take to Britain with him some Gallic chieftains—these would act as good guarantors in his absence from Gaul. One of these, called Dumnorix, refused to comply with his instructions and was killed as he tried to escape.

   Labieno: Titus Labienus was one of the most competent of Caesar's lieutenants in Gaul. Afterwards he defected to Pompey.

4. *gererentur:* subjunctive in an indirect question.

   pro tempore et pro re: Tr. 'as the occasion and circumstance should require'.

7. *leni Africo:* the 'Africus' was the name given to the South-West wind. 'Aquilo' was the North wind, 'Eurus' the East, 'Notus' the South and 'Zephyrus' the West.

   media circiter nocte: ablative of time when.

8. *vento intermisso:* Tr. 'the wind dropped'.

9. *Britanniam relictam:* that would be the cliffs of East Kent.

11. *eam partem:* i.e. probably the coast between Walmer and Deal.

13. *fuit . . . laudanda:* for natural order 'laudanda fuit'.

14. *vectoriis gravibusque navigiis:* instrumental ablative 'in heavily-built . . .'.

15. *accessum est:* note the impersonal use of the verb.

17. *ut:* 'ut' often means 'as' when followed by the indicative.

20. *annotinis:* Tr. 'those built in the previous year'. This word is formed like other words expressing time, e.g. crastinus, diutinus.

   privatis: 'privately owned ships', i.e. those belonging to the officers and traders who accompanied the expedition.

   quisque: 'each'. Often used in a plural sense, 'optimus quisque' —all the best men.

   sui commodi: genitive of purpose. Tr. 'for their own convenience'.

21. *amplius octingentae:* 'amplius' is here strictly adverbial and does not affect the case of 'octingentae'. When used with a numeral the 'quam' is regularly omitted.

22. *se . . . abdiderant:* notice the word order.

   in superiora loca: this probably refers to the high ground near Canterbury overlooking the Great Stour (the river mentioned in the next chapter).

Chapter 8

His rebus gestis, Labieno in continente cum tribus legionibus et equitum milibus duobus relicto, ut portus tueretur et rem frumentariam provideret quaeque in Gallia gererentur cognosceret consiliumque pro tempore et pro re caperet, ipse cum quinque legionibus et pari 5 numero equitum, quem in continenti reliquerat, ad solis occasum naves solvit et leni Africo provectus media circiter nocte vento intermisso cursum non tenuit, et longius delatus aestu orta luce sub sinistra Britanniam relictam conspexit. Tum rursus aestus commutationem secutus 10 remis contendit ut eam partem insulae caperet, qua optimum esse egressum superiore aestate cognoverat. Qua in re admodum fuit militum virtus laudanda, qui vectoriis gravibusque navigiis non intermisso remigandi labore longarum navium cursum adaequarunt. Acces- 15 sum est ad Britanniam omnibus navibus meridiano fere tempore, neque in eo loco hostis est visus; sed, ut postea Caesar ex captivis cognovit, cum magnae manus eo convenissent, multitudine navium perterritae, quae cum annotinis privatisque quas sui quisque commodi 20 fecerat amplius octingentae uno erant visae tempore a litore discesserant ac se in superiora loca abdiderant.

2. *consedissent:* subjunctive in an indirect question.
4. *qui:* final 'qui'.
   praesidio navibus: see note on IV. 20. Tr. 'to guard the fleet'.
5. *veritus navibus:* 'vereor' followed by the dative is a very rare usage.
   in litore molli atque aperto: Tr. 'on a sandy, open shore'. This could certainly apply to the coast near Deal.
7. *praefecit:* this verb takes an accusative of the person (Atrium) and dative of the object commanded (navibus).
10. *flumen:* this could either be the Great or Little Stour, but, as mentioned in the previous chapter, it probably refers to the first of these. R. W. Moore in his book *The Romans in Britain* quotes from Rice Holmes's commentary on Book V:
    'The stronghold to which the Britons retreated was probably a camp in Bigbury Woods, about a mile and half west of Canterbury, of which traces still exist; and it therefore seems most likely that Caesar forced the passage of the river between Canterbury and Thanington'.
13. *ut videbantur* 'as . . .'.
14. *praeparaverant:* the force of the 'prae' means 'beforehand'.
18. *testudine:* this was the name given to a covering formed by legionaries locking their shields together above their heads. In this way they could approach the enemy's walls and undermine them.
    aggere: this was the 'mound' produced by the earth thrown up by the legionaries who undermined the walls. This would enable the storming party to advance.
20. *eos fugientes:* these two words are not to be taken together. 'Eos' is object after 'vetuit' whereas 'fugientes' is dependent on 'prosequi'.

1. *postridie eius diei mane:* this is a good example of pleonasm, i.e. using more words than is really necessary. Simply translate 'on the morning of the next day'.
   tripertito: an adverb 'in three divisions'.
   in expeditionem misit: 'sent as a flying column'. 'Expeditio' here is closely connected with 'miles expeditus'—a light-armed soldier. These would be soldiers sent on a mission which required rapid movement.
3. *aliquantum itineris:* 'some distance'.
   extremi: this refers to the Romans.
5. *nuntiarent:* why is this subjunctive?

Chapter 9

Caesar exposito exercitu et loco castris idoneo capto, ubi
ex captivis cognovit quo in loco hostium copiae consedissent, cohortibus decem ad mare relictis et equitibus
trecentis, qui praesidio navibus essent, de tertia vigilia
ad hostes contendit, eo minus veritus navibus, quod in 5
litore molli atque aperto deligatas ad ancoram relin-
quebat, et praesidio navibus Quintum Atrium praefecit. Ipse noctu progressus milia passuum circiter XII
hostium copias conspicatus est. Illi equitatu atque
essedis ad flumen progressi ex loco superiore nostros 10
prohibere et proelium committere coeperunt. Repulsi
ab equitatu se in silvas abdiderunt, locum nacti egregie
et natura et opere munitum, quem domestici belli, ut
videbantur, causa iam ante praeparaverant: nam cre-
bris arboribus succisis omnes introitus erant praeclusi. 15
Ipsi ex silvis rari propugnabant nostrosque intra munitiones ingredi prohibebant. At milites legionis septimae,
testudine facta et aggere ad munitiones adiecto, locum
ceperunt eosque ex silvis expulerunt paucis vulneribus
acceptis. Sed eos fugientes longius Caesar prosequi 20
vetuit, et quod loci naturam ignorabat, et quod magna
parte diei consumpta munitioni castrorum tempus
relinqui volebat.

Chapter 10

Postridie eius diei mane tripertito milites equitesque in
expeditionem misit, ut eos qui fugerant persequerentur.
His aliquantum itineris progressis, cum iam extremi
essent in prospectu, equites a Quinto Atrio ad Caesarem
venerunt, qui nuntiarent superiore nocte maxima coorta 5

7. *subsisterent:* subjunctive in oratio obliqua.
8. *gubernator:* this is rather an interesting word. Here it simply means 'helmsman' or the 'cox' as in the Varsity Boat Race. However, some writers especially Cicero, the outstanding prose writer of the Classical period, used the word in the plural to mean 'government'. The state was often referred to in poetry as being a ship and a state in trouble was regarded as being buffeted on the waves (*fluctus*).
9. *magnum esse incommodum:* still part of the oratio obliqua.

2. *in itinere resistere:* the Loeb translates 'to keep off attacks on the line of march'.
5. *magno negotio:* 'with great trouble'—an ablative of manner.
6. *fabros:* the legions contained skilled craftsmen (*fabri*) and engineers. They were not recruited into any special corps but were extracted from the various legions when the occasion required them.
8. *eis legionibus:* 'with the help of those legions'.
9. *etsi . . . tamen:* 'etsi' means 'although' and is followed by subjunctive or indicative. After such a clause, the main clause often starts with 'tamen'.
   multae operae ac laboris: a genitive of quality. Tr. 'involving much effort and hard work'.
10. *subduci:* the Romans beached their ships by rolling them on greased rollers. A similar method is employed even today on many of our smaller beaches where slipways are not provided.
12. *ne . . . quidem:* 'not . . . even', and the qualifying words are always inserted between the two Latin words. Tr. 'not even at night'.
18. *Cassivellauno:* he was the chief of a tribe called the Catuvellauni. His territory included the counties of Hertfordshire, Middlesex and Oxfordshire, with the capital at Wheathampstead, a point slightly north of St. Albans.
20. *Tamesis:* the Thames.

tempestate prope omnes naves adflictas atque in litore eiectas esse, quod neque ancorae funesque subsisterent, neque nautae gubernatoresque vim tempestatis pati possent: itaque ex eo concursu navium magnum esse incommodum acceptum. 10

Chapter 11

His rebus cognitis Caesar legiones equitatumque revocari atque in itinere resistere iubet, ipse ad naves revertitur; eadem fere quae ex nuntiis litterisque cognoverat coram perspicit, sic ut amissis circiter XL navibus reliquae tamen refici posse magno negotio viderentur. 5 Itaque ex legionibus fabros deligit et ex continenti alios arcessi iubet; Labieno scribit, ut quam plurimas posset eis legionibus, quae sunt apud eum, naves instituat. Ipse, etsi res erat multae operae ac laboris, tamen commodissimum esse statuit omnes naves subduci et cum 10 castris una munitione coniungi. In his rebus circiter dies X consumit ne nocturnis quidem temporibus ad laborem militum intermissis. Subductis navibus castrisque egregie munitis easdem copias, quas ante, praesidio navibus reliquit: ipse eodem unde redierat proficiscitur. Eo cum 15 venisset, maiores iam undique in eum locum copiae Britannorum convenerant summa imperi bellique administrandi communi consilio permissa Cassivellauno, cuius fines a maritimis civitatibus flumen dividit, quod appellatur Tamesis, a mari circiter milia passuum 20 LXXX. Huic superiore tempore cum reliquis civitatibus continentia bella intercesserant; sed nostro adventu permoti Britanni hunc toti bello imperioque praefecerant.

8.2 94,

ROMAN BRITAIN
Civil & Military
Zones

MILITARY

ZONE

CIVIL

ZONE

Roman Villas

(54)

THE INFLUENCE OF GEOGRAPHICAL FEATURES
ON THE ROMAN OCCUPATION OF BRITAIN

Loca sunt temperatiora quam in Gallia, remissioribus frigoribus.
(Bk. V. 12. 16.)

Britain is divided into two main parts, each with a character of its own, the one a contrast to the other. The first area is to the north and west of a line known as the Tees–Exe line, that is, a line stretching roughly from Middlesborough in the north-east to Exeter in the south-west. Here we have an ancient mountain-chain worn down by ages of erosion into a plateau of hard rock, shattered by the Atlantic weather. The coastline is rugged and irregular and inland there are deep valleys and mountain masses.

The second area is to the south and east of this line and is a plain of newer and softer rocks. These two zones then differ widely in the general character of their landscape. They differ in character of soil. The south and east have fertile soils whereas in the highland zone soils are poor. There is a difference too in climate, 40 inches of rain in the highland zone, 30 inches in the lowland. Furthermore, the areas of lowland which receive the most rain are the chalk plains which rapidly absorb it. These differences in relief, soil and climate have deeply affected the life of the respective inhabitants.

Britain can be divided then into two main areas:

(a) CIVIL ZONE: *this contained the urban centres and villas, and the only fortifications were along the south-east coast.*

(b) MILITARY ZONE: *here forts were strategically positioned —25 in Wales, 30 in Scotland and 70 in northern England. These were to protect the Romanized Zones from the non-Romanized Ireland and Scotland.*

This civil zone, you will now gather, can be identified with

Lowland Britain, that is, all of Britain south and east of the Tees–Exe line, while the military zone embraces Highland Britain.

This area to the south and east comprises downs, meadows, cornlands, all gently contoured. In fact, it is an area relatively easy to conquer. As a result, Caesar on his exploratory expedition, as described in Book IV, advanced to a point west of the Thames without a great deal of trouble, and by A.D. *46, that is, three years after the invasion of Britain was undertaken in earnest by the Emperor Claudius, everything as far as the Fosse Way, that Roman road stretching from Seaton in Devon to Lincoln, was conquered. However, when the governor Agricola came here in* A.D. *78, he found life much more unpalatable because he had to contend with the highland zone which was fringed by heath and forest, poor and rugged by comparison with Lowland Britain, slow to change and certainly slow to yield to conquerors.*

When reading Caesar, it is well worth considering the problems that confronted him and why his advance was rather rapid. It is also worth noting that climatic changes have taken place since post-Glacial times. There has been an improvement in

---

2. *memoria proditum:* understand 'esse'.
3. *ex Belgio:* this must refer to Gallia Belgica, one of the three parts of Gaul. Several of the tribes, settled in Belgica, had sent emigrants across the Channel. Other examples of such offshoots are the Atrebates as mentioned earlier, and the Parisii who dwelt round Paris and round the Humber.
4. *eis nominibus civitatum:* this can be translated as if Caesar had written 'earum nominibus civitatum'.

(56)

climate, a warming-up. Tree cover was very widespread, and nowhere in Britain was free of it—this was confirmed by Caesar who says in Chapter 12 of Book V 'there, as in Gaul, is timber of every description'. All this naturally limited pre-Roman communities to areas which were easy to clear, coastal uplands, chalk and limestone uplands. Communities were isolated from one another by uncleared woodland.

The Military Zone was of great economic significance to the Romans. After agriculture, the most important source of wealth in Britain was her mineral deposits. They were known in Caesar's time (see Chapter 12) and Tacitus, a famous Roman historian, was no doubt well-informed when he said they were among the considerations which prompted the Claudian invasion. In addition to the minerals listed in Chapter 12, there was evidence of lead-mines, gold, coal and copper. It was obvious that Britain could make a material contribution to the Empire's wealth as well as being 'the granary of the north'.

From this brief survey, it is clear that Caesar's invasions were but an exceedingly small forerunner of a much greater invasion under Claudius.

Chapters 12–14
Here we have a description of the people, customs and civilization of Britain.

Chapter 12

Britanniae pars interior ab eis incolitur, quos natos in insula ipsi memoria proditum dicunt, maritima pars ab eis, qui praedae ac belli inferendi causa ex Belgio transierunt (qui omnes fere eis nominibus civitatum appel-

(57)

6. *illato:* from 'infero'.

   permanserunt: notice the force of the compound.

   agros colere: previous inhabitants of Britain had confined themselves to lighter soils. It was the Belgae who settled down to
   clearing large areas of woodland and working the heavier
   soils. They introduced the villa system as mentioned in
   Book IV, chapter 35.

9. *utuntur:* this sentence has given rise to much speculation about
   the coinage which was in use at this time. No bronze coins
   have been found in Britain as early as the invasion of Caesar
   but there were certainly gold coins dating back to 150 B.C.–
   probably debased imitations of the coinage of Philip II of
   Macedon. It would seem that coins began to be struck in
   Britain after the Belgic settlement. Iron rings (*taleis ferreis*)
   have been found in great quantities but not in the south-
   east of Britain which was the most Romanized quarter.
   These seem to have been chiefly used by the south-western
   tribes and probably represent a form of coinage in vogue
   before coinage proper was introduced.

11. *plumbum album:* tin. Caesar says it was mined in the midland
    regions and it would appear that he has been misinformed
    because 'tin' was only mined in Cornwall.

12. *ferrum:* we learn from Strabo, a Greek historian and geo-
    grapher, that iron was already by the time of Augustus
    reckoned an important British product. In the first century,
    iron was worked extensively in the Forest of Dean at Lydney
    and in the Weald. In fact, Sussex was famous for its iron
    until the end of the last century.

    aere . . . importato: there is some doubt here as to whether 'aere'
    means 'copper' or 'bronze'. Copper was apparently ob-
    tained entirely from the Great Orme's Head in Anglesey,
    but there is no evidence that it was mined before Roman
    occupation. There is evidence, however, of bronze being
    produced on a large scale in the Severn valley and Carlisle.
    It could well be that the copper was imported from abroad.

13. *materia:* timber.

14. *praeter fagum:* this seems rather strange because there is con-
    siderable evidence of the existence of beech trees in Britain
    well before Caesar's invasion. The silver-fir (*abies*) was cer-
    tainly imported.

15. *fas:* the very use of this word—it originally belongs to religious
    language—implies that these animals were sacred.

17. *remissioribus frigoribus:* 'the cold being less severe'.

lantur, quibus orti ex civitatibus eo pervenerunt) et 5
bello illato ibi permanserunt atque agros colere coeperunt. Hominum est infinita multitudo creberrimaque
aedificia fere Gallicis consimilia, pecorum magnus
numerus. Utuntur aut aere aut nummo aureo aut taleis
ferreis ad certum pondus examinatis pro nummo. Nasci- 10
tur ibi plumbum album in mediterraneis regionibus, in
maritimis ferrum, sed eius exigua est copia; aere utuntur
importato. Materia cuiusque generis ut in Gallia est,
praeter fagum atque abietem. Leporem et gallinam et
anserem gustare fas non putant; haec tamen alunt 15
animi voluptatisque causa. Loca sunt temperatiora
quam in Gallia, remissioribus frigoribus.

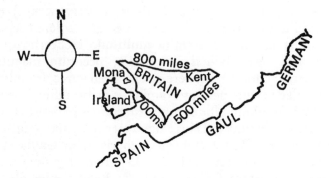

1. *insula natura triquetra:* 'the island was triangular in shape.'
   'natura' is ablative.

   contra Galliam: as can be seen from the map above, Caesar
   imagined that the coast of Gaul and Germany ran parallel
   to one side of Britain.

2. *alter angulus:* this is Kent while 'inferior' refers to Cornwall.
   (Land's End?)

5. *alterum vergit ad Hispaniam:* to say 'the second side faces Spain'
   seems a very bad piece of geography, but in the light of the
   map above the statement is quite feasible.

7. *ut aestimatur:* 'as is thought'.

8. *transmissus:* genitive after 'spatio', 'atque' = 'as'. Tr. 'with the
   same length of crossing as'.

10. *Mona:* this is the regular Latin word for Anglesey, but in this
    context it must mean the Isle of Man.

    complures: Caesar had probably heard from some traders that
    there were other islands farther to the north and this could be
    vague reference to the islands off the west coast of Scotland.

14. *certis ex aqua mensuris:* this refers to measurements made with
    a water-clock, similar to our sand-filled hour-glasses.

16. *illorum:* refers to the 'nonnulli.'

Chapter 13

Insula natura triquetra, cuius unum latus est contra
Galliam. Huius lateris alter angulus, qui est ad Cantium, quo fere omnes ex Gallia naves appelluntur, ad
orientem solem, inferior ad meridiem spectat. Hoc per-
tinet circiter milia passuum quingenta. Alterum vergit 5
ad Hispaniam atque occidentem solem; qua ex parte
est Hibernia, dimidio minor, ut aestimatur, quam
Britannia, sed pari spatio transmissus atque ex Gallia
est in Britanniam. In hoc medio cursu est insula, quae
appellatur Mona: complures praeterea minores subiec- 10
tae insulae existimantur, de quibus insulis nonnulli
scripserunt dies continuos triginta sub bruma esse noc-
tem. Nos nihil de eo percontationibus reperiebamus,
nisi certis ex aqua mensuris breviores esse quam in
continenti noctes videbamus. Huius est longitudo lateris, 15
ut fert illorum opinio, septingentorum milium. Tertium
est contra septentriones; cui parti nulla est obiecta
terra, sed eius angulus lateris maxime ad Germaniam
spectat. Hoc milia passuum octingenta in longitudinem
esse existimatur. Ita omnis insula est in circuitu viciens 20
centum milium passuum.

ANCIENT BRITAIN

Ex his omnibus longe sunt humanissimi qui Cantium incolunt, quae regio est maritima omnis. . . . (Bk. V. 14. 1.)

The student reading Caesar for the first time tends to think of Caesar invading a crude and barren country, where people were clothed in skins and daubed in paint (omnes vero se Britanni vitro inficiunt). This is a complete misconception and this digression sets out to show, brief though it may be, how civilization had developed in Britain before the coming of the Romans.

Life can be traced as far back as Cave man with the final emergence of land-surface from melting ice-fields. These ice-fields had centred principally on highland ground and, when the ice-covering had reached its widest limits, much of the country must have been uninhabitable by man or beast. However, we must pass quickly over this nebulous period, through the Stone Age to something more definite in the form of the Beaker Folk.

The end of the third and the beginning of the second millennia B.C. witnessed considerable movement amongst the peoples of mid-Europe. This was a period of great radical change. Flint was being replaced by metal as the raw material for weapons and tools. The economic and social life of Europe was being subjected to great change and readjustment. Such changes were bound to result in folk movements on a vast scale. The best known of these movements was that of the Beaker Folk. Their distinctive form of pottery—the 'beaker' or 'drinking-cup'—gave rise to this name. Their place of origin was most probably Spain. This movement spread in two directions, north into Brittany and eastwards into Lombardy. In Britain three main types emerged, each type defined by some special physical characteristic. The movements of the Beaker Folk were spasmodic and devious. In Wales, for example, they certainly had a liking for the attractiveness of the coastlands of the north and south.

(62)

There is no indication that they practised agriculture on any considerable scale. They adorned themselves with necklaces. Handled cups of amber and gold have been unearthed in southern England. Many theories have been advanced as to why they came here from the Continent, gold in Ireland being advanced as one of the most plausible. However, it would seem that dissatisfaction with economic change was one of the prime reasons and being a people of sturdy frame their minds were not equipped for such rapid change. This period then accounts for the interval between 2000 and 1500 B.C.

It was the spreading knowledge of the usefulness of copper that brought to an end the Stone Age. The Bronze Age is divided up into three distinct phases and it is phase III, better known as the Late Bronze Age, 1000–400 B.C., that interests us most. In comparison with the Continent, Britain was rather primitive and any progress that emanated was a direct result of invasion from abroad. There was a distinct lack of towns and life was principally confined to isolated farms or hut-villages situated on the light soils. This meant that life in the north and west, the Highland Zone, was perhaps more primitive than in the South and East. However, in contrast to the Early and Middle Bronze Ages, the Late Bronze Age is distinguished by many important changes. Hoards of implements and ornaments now became numerous in all parts of the country. Gold was certainly obtained from Ireland, the El Dorado of the ancient world. In Wales, gold was mined in Merioneth and north Carmarthenshire. Pottery was still made without the wheel and most of the pottery of this period has been recovered from burials. The most outstanding example of this type of craftsmanship was the 'food-vessel' which was found both with inhumation and with incineration burials. It is quite clear that society was now beginning to assume a definite pattern because many of the objects discovered have implied a high degree of wealth.

During the five centuries after 1000 B.C., the so-called

Hallstatt Period, the inhabitants of central Europe learned to use iron increasingly for the manufacture of weapons and tools. This then represents the Early Iron Age. Pottery of the Hallstatt period has not been found west of the Severn, but one enormous hoard of metal objects was found in a lake in North Glamorgan. All these metal objects were characterized by the curvilinear form of decoration which is typical of La Tène or 'Late Celtic' art. Pottery of this period was of a high standard, as were most other objects in wood and metal. In Wales, a most extensive collection of ornamental horse-trappings, tankard handles and other oddments was unearthed near Neath. It included a bronze chisel, two small bells, and a bronze weight which belongs to a non-classical standard. In comparison with their predecessors, these people were organized for warfare and built for themselves hill-forts.

The last invasion of the Iron Age was that of the Belgae who came and settled in Kent, Essex and Hertfordshire. It was a suspicion of these and support for their roots in Gaul that prompted Caesar to undertake his invasion in 55 B.C. Caesar,

---

1. *humanissimi:* 'the most civilized'.
2. *neque multum:* it is worth remembering that inhabitants of Kent eventually were a tribe called the Brythons who came from Belgic Gaul driving the then inhabitants northwards and westwards.
4. *frumenta non serunt:* here Caesar was misinformed because it has been proved archaeologically that corn was grown in Kent from earliest times.
   lacte et carne: instrumental ablatives. Tr. 'live on milk and flesh'.
5. *vitro:* 'woad'. See introduction to this chapter.
6. *hoc:* abl.

in his Commentaries, tells us that king Diviciacus had governed Britain as well as much of north-west Gaul:

'Among them (the Suessiones, a tribe in Gaul) even within living memory, Diviciacus had been king, the most powerful man in the whole of Gaul, who had exercised sovereignty alike over a great part of these districts, and even over Britain.' (Loeb.)

By 75 B.C. or a little later, the Belgae had occupied the territory listed above. It was the Belgae who marked a great stage forward in the civilizing of Britain. Earlier ages had mainly confined themselves to the lighter soils but the Belgae, whose ancestry in part hailed from the forest area of Germany, began to tackle and explore the heavier soils. They came armed with the plough and were ready to cultivate these vast, expansive areas. They brought with them a great advance in pottery and in this field they displayed considerable artistic qualities. They were the first to introduce coinage into Britain. The Belgae had a marked influence on the course of affairs and it was little wonder that Caesar felt a great need to come to this island and seek out such an advanced tribe.

15.2.94.

Chapter 14

Ex his omnibus longe sunt humanissimi qui Cantium incolunt, quae regio est maritima omnis, neque multum a Gallica differunt consuetudine. Interiores plerique frumenta non serunt, sed lacte et carne vivunt pellibusque sunt vestiti. Omnes vero se Britanni vitro inficiunt, quod caeruleum efficit colorem, atque hoc horridiores sunt in pugna aspectu; capilloque sunt promisso atque omni parte corporis rasa praeter caput et labrum

5

9. *deni duodenique:* it is fairly certain that this practice was not common throughout Britain. This custom is still held among certain Orientals but it is extremely rare among Aryan tribes. It was the Aryan family which drove the Celts to the extreme corners of the British Isles and it could well be a reference to these far-flung areas!

2. *ut . . . fuerint:* note the perfect subjunctive in a consecutive clause. This is used when it is desired to emphasize the fact or stress the actuality of the result.

5. *illi:* i.e. the Britons.

9. *subsidio:* for the use of this dative see the note on IV, 20.
10. *eis primis legionum duarum:* 'those the first cohorts of two legions'. The first cohort would be the best and would contain picked men.
11. *perexiguo:* note the force of the compound. 'Exiguus' = small, 'perexiguus' = very small.

15. *tribunus militum:* see introduction to chapter 8 of Book V.

superius. Uxores habent deni duodenique inter se communes et maxime fratres cum fratribus parentesque [10] cum liberis; sed qui sunt ex his nati, eorum habentur liberi, quo primum virgo quaeque deducta est.

Chapters 15–17

Caesar then advanced and although he repulsed the Britons, he was again attacked and lost one of his officers. The Romans were encountering difficulties in coping with the guerrilla tactics of the Britons. The Britons attacked a foraging party but were routed by the Romans.

Chapter 15

Equites hostium essedariique acriter proelio cum equitatu nostro in itinere conflixerunt, tamen ut nostri omnibus partibus superiores fuerint atque eos in silvas collesque compulerint; sed compluribus interfectis cupidius insecuti nonnullos ex suis amiserunt. At illi 5 intermisso spatio imprudentibus nostris atque occupatis in munitione castrorum subito se ex silvis eiecerunt impetuque in eos facto qui erant in statione pro castris collocati, acriter pugnaverunt, duabusque missis subsidio cohortibus a Caesare atque eis primis legionum [10] duarum, cum hae perexiguo intermisso loci spatio inter se constitissent, novo genere pugnae perterritis nostris per medios audacissime perruperunt seque inde incolumes receperunt. Eo die Quintus Laberius Durus, tribunus militum, interficitur. Illi pluribus submissis [15] cohortibus repelluntur.

2. *dimicaretur/intellectum est:* note the impersonal use of these verbs.
4. *ab signis discedere auderent:* Tr. 'nor did they dare to venture far from the standards'—simply because they were armed for fighting in close formation.
7. *consulto:* adverb. Cf. 'tripartito' in V, 10.
9. *equestris:* this sentence is difficult and the meaning is obscure. It would appear that the chariots made a charge against the enemy and the men leaping down would fight it out while the chariots withdrew a little and waited for the fighters if they were beaten or to receive them as victors. Translate here—'their cavalry tactics, however, threatened us with exactly the same danger in retirement or pursuit'. (Loeb.)
11. *accedebat:* another use of the impersonal. Tr. 'there is the further fact that . . .'.
14. *integrique et recentes:* 'and so untired and fresh'. This is a common idiom in the best Latin prose. When something important needs to be stressed, the best Latin authors would use two words which express the same idea, as here. Another example is *'oro et obsecro'*—I beg and pray of you.

1. *constiterunt:* note the principal parts of this verb.
2. *lenius:* 'with less vigour'.
4. *pabulandi causa:* 'for the sake of foraging'. Note here that when 'causa' takes the genitive of the gerund, it always comes after the verb.
5. *Gaio Trebonio:* he was a distinguished 'legatus' throughout this war and had held several important posts under Caesar during the Civil Wars. Yet he was one of the chief instigators in the murder of Caesar but soon he was to suffer death at the hands of Dolabella after he had secured the governorship of Asia.
8. *finem sequendi:* a genitive of the gerund depending on 'finis'.
9. *quoad:* 'until'.
   subsidio: ablative case after 'confisi', a regular usage when things are concerned: otherwise a dative is common.

15. *summis copiis:* 'with their full strength'. Ablative of manner.

Chapter 16

Toto hoc in genere pugnae, cum sub oculis omnium ac pro castris dimicaretur, intellectum est nostros propter gravitatem armorum, quod neque insequi cedentes possent neque ab signis discedere auderent, minus aptos esse ad huius generis hostem, equites autem magno cum 5 periculo proelio dimicare, propterea quod illi etiam consulto plerumque cederent et, cum paulum ab legionibus nostros removissent, ex essedis desilirent et pedibus dispari proelio contenderent. Equestris autem proeli ratio et cedentibus et insequentibus par atque 10 idem periculum inferebat. Accedebat huc ut numquam conferti sed rari magnisque intervallis proeliarentur stationesque dispositas haberent, atque alios alii deinceps exciperent, integrique et recentes defatigatis succederent.

Chapter 17

Postero die procul a castris hostes in collibus constiterunt rarique se ostendere et lenius quam pridie nostros equites proelio lacessere coeperunt. Sed meridie, cum Caesar pabulandi causa tres legiones atque omnem equitatum cum Gaio Trebonio legato misisset, repente 5 ex omnibus partibus ad pabulatores advolaverunt, sic uti ab signis legionibusque non absisterent. Nostri acriter in eos impetu facto reppulerunt neque finem sequendi fecerunt, quoad subsidio confisi equites, cum post se legiones viderent, praecipites hostes egerunt magnoque 10 eorum numero interfecto neque sui colligendi neque consistendi aut ex essedis desiliendi facultatem dederunt. Ex hac fuga protinus, quae undique convenerant, auxilia discesserunt, neque post id tempus umquam summis nobiscum copiis hostes contenderunt.

2. *uno omnino loco pedibus:* no one knows where this spot exactly was. However, it is generally accepted that it was either at Coway Stakes (Walton-on-Thames) or Brentford. Bede, an English monk known as 'the father of English learning' relates that the stakes were still visible in his day (673–735). There is a stake in the Gunnersbury Park Museum at Brentford.

4. *animum advertit:* these two words are often written as one word 'animadverto'.

6. *praefixis/defixae:* note the force of the compounds.

8. *praemisso equitatu:* this does not mean that the cavalry were sent across at this point where the stakes were but rather at a more suitable spot farther downstream.

10. *cum:* here 'cum' has a concessive force 'although'.

Caesar advanced towards the Thames and the terri-
tories of Cassivellaunus. Cassivellaunus avoided a
pitched battle but harassed Caesar's army on the
march. The Trinobantes, followed soon by other tribes,
surrendered to Caesar. Caesar captured a stronghold of
Cassivellaunus and inflicted considerable losses. Cassivellaunus then managed to persuade four Kentish kings
to attack Caesar's naval camp but the attempt failed
miserably. Terms were then agreed between the two
opponents. Caesar returned to Gaul with many captives.

Chapter 18

Caesar cognito consilio eorum ad flumen Tamesim in
fines Cassivellauni exercitum duxit; quod flumen uno
omnino loco pedibus, atque hoc aegre, transiri potest.
Eo cum venisset, animum advertit ad alteram fluminis
ripam magnas esse copias hostium instructas. Ripa 5
autem erat acutis sudibus praefixis munita, eiusdemque
generis sub aqua defixae sudes flumine tegebantur. His
rebus cognitis a captivis perfugisque Caesar praemisso
equitatu confestim legiones subsequi iussit. Sed ea
celeritate atque eo impetu milites ierunt, cum capite 10
solo ex aqua exstarent, ut hostes impetum legionum
atque equitum sustinere non possent ripasque dimit-
terent ac se fugae mandarent.

23.2.94.

1. *Cassivellaunus, ut supra:* the first sentence here is a fine example of what is called 'period' writing. When translating from English into Latin, it will be found that a more satisfactory Latin will be written if a series of several English sentences are combined into a single period. This is readily achieved in Latin by frequent use of subordination, use of participles, ablative absolutes. When translating the latter, great care should be taken not to translate them literally (e.g. 'having been'), but make use of subordinate clauses. It would be advisable to break this sentence down into much smaller units. The use of the imperfect tense here denotes repeated action.

7. *cum:* has a frequentative sense 'whenever'.

9. *omnibus viis semitisque:* 'by every road and path'. Ablative of road by which'.

11. *hoc metu:* Tr. 'through fear of this'.

13. *discedi/noceretur:* further uses of the impersonal.

1. *Trinobantes:* a powerful tribe which occupied parts of Essex and Suffolk. They bitterly resented Cassivellaunus because he had murdered their king, and their willingness to co-operate with Caesar crippled the resistance of the patriots to the Romans. Their capital was Camulodunum (Colchester).

9. *qui praesit:* the antecedent to 'qui' is omitted. The mood of 'praesit' and 'obtineat' is due to the final sense of the clause.

Chapter 19

Cassivellaunus, ut supra demonstravimus, omni deposita spe contentionis dimissis amplioribus copiis milibus circiter quattuor essedariorum relictis itinera nostra servabat paulumque ex via excedebat locisque impeditis ac silvestribus sese occultabat, atque eis regionibus 5 quibus nos iter facturos cognoverat pecora atque homines ex agris in silvas compellebat et, cum equitatus noster liberius praedandi vastandique causa se in agros eiecerat, omnibus viis semitisque essedarios ex silvis emittebat et magno cum periculo nostrorum equitum 10 cum eis confligebat atque hoc metu latius vagari prohibebat. Relinquebatur ut neque longius ab agmine legionum discedi Caesar pateretur, et tantum in agris vastandis incendiisque faciendis hostibus noceretur, quantum labore atque itinere legionarii milites efficere 15 poterant.

Chapter 20

Interim Trinobantes, prope firmissima earum regionum civitas, ex qua Mandubracius adulescens Caesaris fidem secutus ad eum in continentem Galliam venerat, cuius pater in ea civitate regnum obtinuerat interfectusque erat a Cassivellauno, ipse fuga mortem vitaverat, 5 legatos ad Caesarem mittunt pollicenturque sese ei dedituros atque imperata facturos; petunt, ut Mandubracium ab iniuria Cassivellauni defendat atque in civitatem mittat, qui praesit imperiumque obtineat. His Caesar imperat obsides quadraginta frumentumque 10 exercitui Mandubraciumque ad eos mittit. Illi imperata celeriter fecerunt, obsides ad numerum frumentumque miserunt.

2. *Cenimagni:* virtually nothing is known about these tribes. They probably lived around the Thames basin.

6. *oppidum:* this does not mean a walled town but in *Caesar* it is regularly used of a stronghold. It was in effect a stockade with its usual ditch and rampart. The site could well have been that of St. Albans.

11. *oppugnare contendit:* 'oppugnare' is a prolative infinitive. Prolative is derived from a Latin verb 'profero' which means 'I carry forward': hence the infinitive 'carries forward' the meaning of verbs that are incomplete in themselves.

2. *supra:* this refers to chapter 14.

11. *per Atrebatem:* it would appear that this was done at Caesar's suggestion and that the overtures first came from Caesar himself as he was anxious to return to Gaul.

(74)

Chapter 21

Trinobantibus defensis atque ab omni militum iniuria prohibitis Cenimagni, Segontiaci, Ancalites, Bibroci, Cassi legationibus missis sese Caesari dedunt. Ab his cognoscit non longe ex eo loco oppidum Cassivellauni abesse silvis paludibusque munitum, quo satis magnus 5 hominum pecorisque numerus convenerit. Oppidum autem Britanni vocant, cum silvas impeditas vallo atque fossa munierunt, quo incursionis hostium vitandae causa convenire consuerunt. Eo proficiscitur cum legionibus: locum reperit egregie natura atque opere 10 munitum; tamen hunc duabus ex partibus oppugnare contendit. Hostes paulisper morati militum nostrorum impetum non tulerunt seseque alia ex parte oppidi eiecerunt. Magnus ibi numerus pecoris repertus, multique in fuga sunt comprehensi atque interfecti.

Chapter 22

Dum haec in his locis geruntur, Cassivellaunus ad Cantium, quod esse ad mare supra demonstravimus, quibus regionibus quattuor reges praeerant, Cingetorix, Carvilius, Taximagulus, Segovax, nuntios mittit atque eis imperat uti coactis omnibus copiis castra navalia de 5 improviso adoriantur atque oppugnent. Ei cum ad castra venissent, nostri eruptione facta multis eorum interfectis, capto etiam nobili duce Lugotorige suos incolumes reduxerunt. Cassivellaunus hoc proelio nuntiato tot detrimentis acceptis, vastatis finibus, maxime 10 etiam permotus defectione civitatum, legatos per Atrebatem Commium de deditione ad Caesarem mittit. Caesar, cum constituisset hiemare in continenti propter

(75)

14. *multum aestatis:* a partitive genitive 'much of the summer'.
15. *id facile extrahi:* Tr. 'it might be easily spun out'.
16. *vectigalis:* this was the term applied to any tax especially to that paid by the provincials and other conquered peoples. It also included tithes for public lands and port dues. In this particular context the tax or tribute was never paid.
18. *Mandubracio/Trinobantibus:* indirect objects after 'noceat'.

2. *deductis:* 'launched'.

4. *duobus commeatibus:* 'in two trips'.

11. *perpaucae:* '*very* few'.
12. *quas:* a connecting relative.
13. *exspectasset:* for 'exspectavisset'.
14. *aequinoctium:* from this it would appear that Caesar left towards the end of September (the time of the autumnal equinox). Seeing that he probably arrived in Britain about the middle of July, his stay lasted for about ten weeks.

repentinos Galliae motus, neque multum aestatis super-
esset, atque id facile extrahi posse intellegeret, obsides 15
imperat et quid in annos singulos vectigalis populo
Romano Britannia penderet constituit; interdicit atque
imperat Cassivellauno, ne Mandubracio neu Trinobantibus noceat.

Chapter 23

Obsidibus acceptis exercitum reducit ad mare, naves
invenit refectas. His deductis, quod et captivorum
magnum numerum habebat, et nonnullae tempestate
deperierant naves, duobus commeatibus exercitum re-
portare instituit. Ac sic accidit, uti ex tanto navium 5
numero tot navigationibus neque hoc neque superiore
anno ulla omnino navis, quae milites portaret, desi-
deraretur; at ex eis, quae inanes ex continenti ad eum
remitterentur et prioris commeatus expositis militibus
et quas postea Labienus faciendas curaverat numero 10
LX, perpaucae locum caperent, reliquae fere omnes
reicerentur. Quas cum aliquamdiu Caesar frustra
exspectasset, ne anni tempore a navigatione excludere-
tur, quod aequinoctium suberat, necessario angustius
milites collocavit ac summa tranquillitate consecuta, 15
secunda inita cum solvisset vigilia, prima luce terram
attigit omnesque incolumes naves perduxit.

Oppidum autem Britanni vocant, cum silvas impeditas vallo atque fossa munierunt. . . . (Bk. V. 21. 6.)

Dwellers around the Mediterranean, the seat of early civilization, were essentially town-dwellers. Politically and socially the Mediterranean way of life depended on the life of the town. In ancient Greece, life centred around the πόλις, the city-state, and in the Roman world citizenship of Rome was a much-coveted honour. Julius Caesar, on his second visit to Britain, could not help but compare the ancient Britons' concept of 'oppidum' with the Roman idea and he summed it up—'now the Britons call it a stronghold (town!) when they have fortified a thick-set woodland with rampart and trench, and thither it is their custom to collect. . . .' The town was the method by which the Romans tried to introduce civilization. The Romans would introduce it by means of the aristocratic families and urge them to become Roman citizens.

How did the Romans tackle this mammoth task? They took over existing urban centres like Colchester and St. Albans, although these were not very populous. They developed their regional capitals on the line of the scarp—at Wroxeter, Exeter and Dorchester. Here, as in the case of Dorchester, the hill-top towns of the earlier period—Maiden Castle—had now moved down into the valleys. The Romans next developed their most important military towns at the junction of the two zones, that is the Lowland and Highland. Such towns were Lincoln, York, Chester, Gloucester, Caerleon. They established their market towns at important road junctions where food from the villas could be sold—such towns were Bath, Cirencester, Cambridge, Carlisle. Finally they established London as their main contact with the Continent. This was to be their commercial centre, their true emporium. It is significant how even today the same towns

(78)

exist and London is now the great link with Europe. Here I would quote Professor Richmond who admirably sums up the wisdom behind the choice of London as the link with Europe:

> *'Nature here contained the tidal Thames within hard gravel banks and made possible the construction of a bridge, where land traffic and sea traffic for the whole islands met. The roads radiated from the bridge head, the sea lanes converged upon it from the Rhine, the Gallic coastal ports, and the North Sea or by the Channel route from Bordeaux, Spain and the Mediterranean. No question of status could prevent Londinium from becoming the natural centre for British trade and administration once the Roman engineers had picked it.'*

How history has approved their choice!

Let us examine the site, structure and development of a Roman town. Caerwent (*Venta Silurum*) is situated on the Monmouthshire plain. Not far away were the customary hill-forts of the earlier period. The Roman road from Gloucester (*Glevum*) to Caerleon (*Isca Silurum*) passed through it. It was one of the smallest Roman towns and its total acreage was $44\frac{1}{2}$ acres. The town was erected in A.D. 80 when the Silures, a name given to a tribe which inherited what is now South Wales, were defeated. It seems to have been furnished with an earthen bank surrounded by two ditches, the inner ditch being slightly larger. At a later stage the earthen bank received a stone wall, *10 feet* wide at the foundations but reduced by offsets to a width of *6 feet*. The South wall has actually shown how the wall was erected.

The main road, *'decumanus maximus'* is clearly marked, as also are the two other roadways known as *'decumani'* (*E–W*) and *'cardines'* (*N–S*). The *'decumanus maximus'* was *40 feet* wide with side-walks while the others were *10 feet* wide. In the centre of the town were the forum and the basilica. The forum was the market-place and was entered through a colonnaded *portico and then an ornamental arch. Ambulatories ran round three sides. The basilica was colonnaded.*

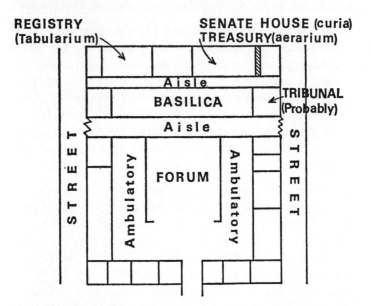

REGISTRY (Tabularium)

SENATE HOUSE (curia)
TREASURY(aerarium)

Aisle

BASILICA

TRIBUNAL (Probably)

Aisle

STREET

Ambulatory

FORUM

Ambulatory

STREET

Public baths were always provided in every capital. There was the elaborate peristyled entrance and the courtyard. There was evidence for the continued occupation of the bath building up to the beginning of the third century. On the other side of the forum was a temple which was entered through a small chamber with an apse on one side. A portice ran round the whole building. An amphitheatre was unearthed at Caerwent but so far there is no evidence of seating accommodation.

There was quite a variety of private buildings. At Caerwent about sixty-five have been uncovered. They were aligned in rows along the streets and usually a space was left behind them where refuse-pits could be dug. The houses were of three types, similar to those of the villas as described on page 40.

(80)

(a) *The strip-house was a long rectangular building, with the narrow end facing the street. It had a gabled roof and was clearly single-storied. It represents the poorest inhabitants of the town.*

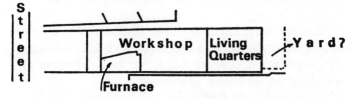

(b) *The corridor plan probably belonged to the bureaucratic class.*

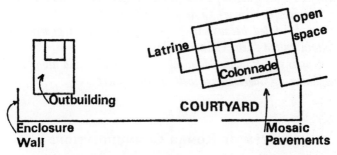

(c) *The courtyard house was large, well-equipped and probably was the town residence of the tribal magnate.*

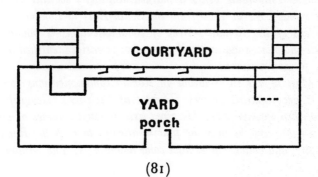

The strip house and corridor plan are typical of the Romano-Celtic type, whereas the courtyard house has affinities with the Graeco-Roman type of house.

Caerwent had two to three thousand inhabitants. There was a reasonable water supply and about twenty wells have been found.

Three important inscriptions were discovered, among which one was rather significant in that it mentions 'civitas Silurum', and furthermore it mentions that it has been recognized as a 'respublica' by the Roman government.

'Ti(berio) Claudio Paulino leg(ato) Leg(ionis) I(I) Augustae Proconsul(i) provinc(iae) Narbonensis Leg(ato) Aug(usti) Pr(o) Pr(aetore) Provi(ncias) Lugdamen(sis) ex decreto/ ordinis Res/publ(icae) Civit(atis) Silurum.'

It can be dated because in 217–219 we have a governor of Britain called Tib. Claudius Paulinus.

Remains of Roman Caerwent are still visible and along with neighbouring Caerleon are well worth a visit.

SYSTEM OF ROMAN COMMUNICATIONS

Caesar, after landing at a point somewhere near Dover, made his advance as far as the Thames and the territory of Cassivellaunus. This route bears a marked similarity to that of our present-day A2 or A20 from the South-East to London. Any student of the Roman system of communications is bound to notice how our road and rail routes can be easily identified with the Roman network.

Most of our information on Roman communications comes from geographical sources. There was Ptolemy's 'Geography' published in A.D. 120. He gives lists of towns, names of seas and tribes and he was the first to attempt to map the Roman empire, and actual names have come down to us. The 'Antonine

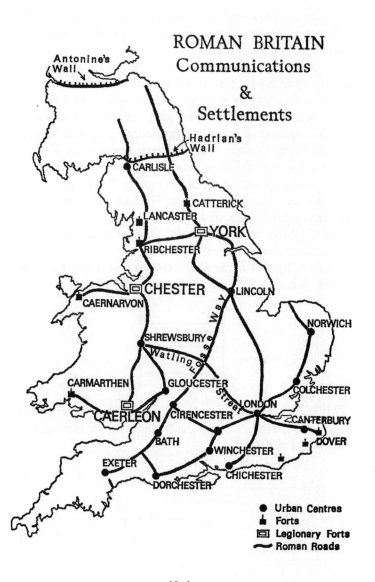

ROMAN BRITAIN
Communications
&
Settlements

Antonine's Wall

Hadrian's Wall

CARLISLE

CATTERICK

LANCASTER

YORK

RIBCHESTER

CHESTER

LINCOLN

CAERNARVON

NORWICH

SHREWSBURY

Watling Street

Fosse Way

CARMARTHEN

GLOUCESTER

COLCHESTER

CAERLEON

CIRENCESTER

LONDON

CANTERBURY

BATH

WINCHESTER

DOVER

EXETER

CHICHESTER

DORCHESTER

● Urban Centres
▲ Forts
▣ Legionary Forts
〜 Roman Roads

Itinerary', a road book published round about A.D 211, provides us with but scant information. Thirdly, there is the obvious source of literature.

It is clear that one of the main reasons for the spread of Roman civilization was excellent road communication. The roads were primarily military and strategic, they represented the actual line of the Roman conquest and were also used as the essential network of quick communication. They have two outstanding characteristics, their directness and solidity. The road system suggests a swiftness and certitude of mind which was one of the main reasons for the success of the Roman people. The most striking example is the Fosse Way which ran from Seaton in Devon north-eastwards to Lincoln.

It is notable how the Romans made use of natural physical features for their communications. In northern England, the routes ran parallel to the Pennines with links through the gaps in the upland:

This is very similar to our present-day network of communications. In Scotland, the major route was along the east coast and then across country.

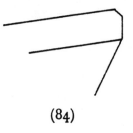

In Wales, too, the organization of the defensive scheme was governed by the geography of the region. The dominant feature of the Welsh land surface is its hills. The scheme of defence applied by the Romans to this region comprised the usual elements of any occupation—base fortresses (*castra*), advance forts (*castella*), and a network of interconnecting roads (*limites*). Chester (*Deva*) in the north and Caerleon (*Isca*) in the south formed the legionary bases and from them strategic roads, policed by intermediate forts, were pushed forward by way of river valleys into the heart of the mountainous Welsh hinterland and along the coastal fringes. The Romans moved along the Vale of Glamorgan in the south to Carmarthen and along the north coast route to Caernarvon. Even today the A48 in South Wales follows the same line, as does the A55 along the north coast. As a result, the Welsh frontier system took the shape of a quadrilateral with the angles at Chester, Caerleon, Carmarthen and Caernarvon and the interior was strengthened with a complex of valley roads and forts.

The road had four main stages in its make-up. At the bottom was the smooth bed, a layer of large stones. Above this came a layer of rubble on top of which there was a stratum of concrete. Finally there was the paving. In Britain there was a great variety of roads but in general the paved road was out of favour. There were usually short, straight sectors. Bends were angular rather than curved. The road was usually raised up on a small causeway from 6 to 21 feet wide and on either side would be two small ditches. In hill country, like the Lake District, the road zigzagged in short, angular sections. The Romans forded rivers and between Newcastle and Carlisle there is an example of four Roman bridges. The roads were furnished at 25-mile intervals with small stopping places where horses could be changed, refreshment and accommodation obtained. These were important posts but do not appear in military areas—instead they are replaced by the forts themselves. From literature we

(85)

ROMAN WALES
Roads & Settlements

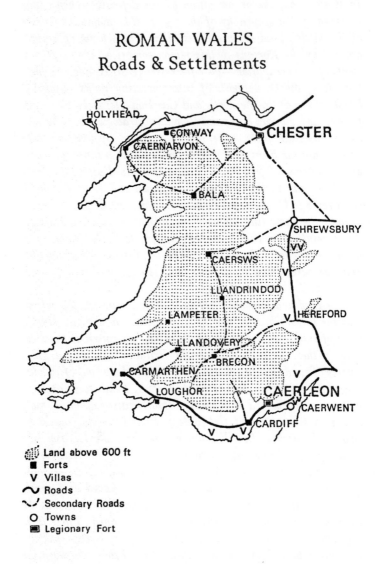

Land above 600 ft
■ Forts
V Villas
~ Roads
~✓ Secondary Roads
○ Towns
▦ Legionary Fort

(86)

learn that for very fast moving the Romans used the two-wheeled chariot, whereas for heavy traffic it was the four-wheeled carriage or even sometimes the cart. In towns the wealthy had litters and for long distance a carriage, while the poor had to walk or travel by mule. The maintenance of the Roman roads was shared: the imperial highways were under the care of the Emperor, while the small roads were maintained by the tribal system of local government.

All this is known from the evidence of mile-stones. From Wales, thirteen mile-stones were found—they tell us two things. They might give an indication of the distance from any given place and also the name of that place. A stone was found with the inscription:

... milium passuum Ratae ...

this gives us the name of the town of Leicester. They also set up the name of the particular emperor responsible for the erection of a particular road.

VOCABULARY

a, ab (prep. w. abl.): from, by, on the side of,
abdo, -ere, -didi, -ditum: to hide, conceal
abeo, -ire, -ii, -itum: to go away, depart
abies, -etis (f): a fir-tree
absisto, -ere, -stiti, -stitum: to desist, stop short
ac (conj.): and (emphatic)
accedo, -ere, -cessi, -cessum: to approach, advance
accido, -ere, -cidi: to happen
accipio, -ere, -cepi, -ceptum: to receive, learn
acriter, acrius, acerrime (adv.): fiercely, vigorously
acutus, -a, -um: sharp, pointed
ad (prep. w. acc.): to, towards, up to, by, near, for the purpose of
adaequo, -are, -avi, -atum: to make equal, to equal
adduco, -ere, -xi, -ctum: to lead, bring to, induce
adeo, -ire, -ii, -itum: to go towards, approach
adeo (adv.): so, to such an extent
adflicto, -are, -avi, -atum: to damage, wreck, buffet
adgrego, -are, -avi, -atum: to gather round, join
adicio, -ere, -ieci, -iectum: to throw up against
adigo, -ere, -egi, -actum: to push up, hurl against
aditus, -us (m): approach, access
administro, -are, -avi, -atum: to perform, manage, carry out
admitto, -ere, -misi, -missum: to commit (a crime), incur (disgrace), let go
admodum (adv.): very, quite, greatly, much
adorior, -oriri, -ortus sum: to attack
adulescens, -tis (m): youth
adventus, -us (m): approach
adversus, -a, -um: opposite, unfavourable
adverto, -ere, -verti, -versum: to turn towards
advolo, -are, -avi, -atum: to rush at, swoop upon
aedificium, -i (n): building
aeger, -gra, -grum: ill, sick
aegre, -rius, -aegerrime (adv.): scarcely, with difficulty
aequinoctium, -i (n): equinox, time of equal days and nights

(89)

aes, aeris (n): copper, bronze
aestas, -atis (f): summer
aestimo, -are, -avi, -atum: to weigh, value, assess
aestus, -us (m): heat, tide, current
Africus, -i (m): south-west wind
ager, -gri (m): land, field, territory
agger, -eris (m): rampart, mound, material
agmen, -inis (n): column, army
ago, -ere, egi, actum: to do, drive
alacer, -cris, -cre: keen, eager
alacritas, -atis (f): keenness, enthusiasm
aliquamdiu (adv.): for a considerable time
aliquantus, -a, -um: considerable
aliqui, -qua, -quod: some
aliquis, -quis, -quid (indef. pron.): some one, something
alius, -a, -ud: other, different
alo, -ere, -ui, altum: to feed, support
alter, -a, -um: one or other of two
altitudo, -inis (f): height, depth
altus, -a -um: high, deep; **altum**: deep water
amitto, -ere, -misi, -missum: to lose
amplius (comp. adv.): more, farther
an (conj.): or
Ancalites, -um (m): a British tribe
ancora, -ae (f): anchor
angulus, -i (m): angle, corner
angustus, -a, -um: narrow, close together, scanty
animadverto, -ere, -verti, -versum: to notice, perceive
animus, -i (m): feeling, courage, desire, purpose
annotinus, -a, -um: last year's, a year old
annus, -i (m): a year
anser, -eris (m): a goose
ante (prep. w. acc.): before; (adv.) previously
antepono, -ere, -posui, -positum: to place before, prefer
aperio, -ire, -ui, pertum: to open, disclose; **apertus**: open
appello, -are, -avi, -atum: to call, name
appropinquo, -are, -avi, -atum: to approach, come near
aptus, -a, -um: fit, suitable
apud (prep. w. acc.): near, in the presence of, among
aqua, -ae (f): water
aquila, -ae (f): eagle, standard

arbitror, -ari, arbitratus sum: to consider, believe, judge
arbor, -oris (f): tree
arcesso, -ere, -ivi, -itum: to summon
aridus, -a, -um: dry; **aridum:** the dry land
arma, -orum (n. pl.): arms, weapons
armamenta, -orum (n): fittings, tackle
armo, -are, -avi, -atum: to arm, equip
aspectus, -us (m): sight, appearance
at (conj.): but, yet
atque, ac (conj.): and (emphatic)
Atrebas, -atis (m): an Atrebatian, a member of the Atrebates
attingo, -ere, -tigi, -tactum: to reach, touch
attribuo, -ere, -ui, -utum: to assign
auctoritas, -atis (f): influence, authority
audacter, audacius, audacissime (adv.): boldly
audax, -cis: daring, bold
audeo, -ēre, ausus sum: to dare, venture
audio, -ire, -ivi, -itum: to hear
aureus, -a, -um: golden
auriga, -ae (m): charioteer, driver
aut (conj.): or; **aut . . . aut:** either . . . or
autem (conj.): however, but
autumnus, -i (m): autumn
auxilior, -ari, -atus sum: to bring assistance
auxilium, -i (n): help

barbarus, -i (m): native, foreigner
barbarus, -a, -um: uncivilized, foreign
bellum, -i (n): war
Bibroci, -orum (m): a British tribe
brevis, -e: short
Britanni, -orum (m): the Britons
Britannia, -ae (f): Britain
bruma, -ae (f): the shortest day, winter

caeruleus, -a, -um: dark blue-green
campus, -i (m): a plain
Cantium, -i (n): Kent
capillus, -i (m): hair
capio, -ere, -cepi, -captum: to take, capture, receive
captivus, -i (m): prisoner, captive

(91)

caput, -itis (n): head
caro, carnis (f): flesh
Cassi, -orum (m. pl.): a British tribe
Cassivellaunus, -i (m): chief of a Belgic tribe in Britain
castra, -orum (n. pl.): camp
casus, -us (m): chance, event, result, emergency
causa, -ae (f): cause, reason; gen. +**causa**: for the sake of
cedo, -ere, cessi, cessum: to yield, retreat
celer, -eris, -ere: fast, swift, rapid
celeritas, -atis (f): swiftness, speed
celeriter, celerius, celerrime (adv.): quickly
Cenimagni, -orum (m. pl.): a British tribe
centum: a hundred
certe (adv.): certainly, undoubtedly, at any rate
certus, -a, -um: sure, certain
Cingetorix, -igis (m): one of the four kings of Kent
circiter (prep. w. acc.): about, around
circuitus, -us (m): circuit, detour, circumference
circum (prep. w. acc.): near, about, around
circumdo, -are, -dedi, -datum: to put round, encircle, surround
circumsisto, -ere, -steti: to surround, stand around
citissime (sup. adv.): very quickly
civitas, -atis (f): state, community
clam (adv.): secretly
classis, -is (f): a fleet
coepi, -isse: to have begun
cognosco, -ere, -ovi, -nitum: to get to know, discover
cogo, -ere, coegi, coactum: to compel, collect
cohors, -tis (f): cohort
cohortor, -ari, -atus sum: to encourage, urge
coicio, -ere; conieci, coniectum: to throw, hurl
colligo, -ere, collegi, collectum: to collect, rally, concentrate
collis, -is (m): hill
colloco, -are, -avi, -atum: to post, station, place
colo, -ere, -ui, cultum: to cultivate
color, -oris (m): colour
commeatus, -us (m): passage, supplies
commendo, -are, -avi, -atum: to trust, hand over
committo, -ere, -misi, -missum: to entrust, join (battle)
Commius, -i (m): chief of the Atrebates, a British tribe

commodum, -i (n): advantage, profit
commodus, -a, -um: advantageous, convenient
commode (adv.): conveniently, adequately
communis, -e: common, general, shared
commutatio, -onis (f): a change
comparo, -are, -avi, -atum: to prepare, compare
compello, -ere, -puli, -pulsum: to drive together
compleo, -ēre, evi, -etum: to fill up, man
complures, -ium: several
comporto, -are, -avi, -atum: to carry, bring together, collect
comprehendo, -ere, -di, sum: to arrest, seize
concursus, -us (m): a thronging, collision
confero, -ferre, contuli, conlatum: to bring together
confertus, -a, -um (from **confercio**): closely-packed, crowded
confestim (adv.): immediately
confido, -ere, -fisus sum: to trust, rely on; w. dat. or abl. be confident
confirmo, -are, -avi, -atum: to strengthen, secure, reinforce, affirm
confligo, -ere, -flixi, -flictum: to fight, engage with
coniungo, -ere, -iunxi, -iunctum: to join together, unite
coniuratio, -onis (f): conspiracy
conloquor, -i, -locutus sum: to hold a conference, parley
conscendo, -ere, -endi, -ensum: to climb, embark, mount
consequor, -i, -secutus sum: to pursue, chase, follow
consido, -ere, -sedi, -sessum: to encamp, take up a position
consilium, -i (n): plan, council of war
consimilis, -e: similar, like
consisto, -ere, -stiti, -stitum: to stand, keep one's position
conspicio, -ere, -spexi, -spectum: to see, catch sight of
conspicor, -ari, -atus sum: to catch sight of, observe
constituo, -ere, -ui, -utum: to draw up, fix, resolve, decide
consto, -are, -stiti: to be established; **constat:** it is agreed
consuesco, -ere, -suevi, -suetum: to grow accustomed
consuetudo, -inis (f): a custom
consulto (adv.): deliberately, on purpose
consumo, -ere, -sumpsi, -sumptum: to use up, waste, spend time
contendo, -ere, -di, -tum: to hurry, fight, strive
contestor, -ari, -atus sum: to call to witness
continens, -entis: the mainland

(93)

contineo, -ēre, -ui, -tentum: to limit, bound, confine, include

continuus, -a, -um: successive, consecutive

contra (prep. w. acc.): against, facing, contrary to; (adv.) opposite

contraho, -ere, -traxi, -tractum: to drag together, summon together

convenio, -ire, -veni, -ventum: to come together, meet, assemble

convoco, -are, -avi, -atum: to call together, to summon together

coorior, -iri, -ortus sum: to arise, break out

copia, -ae (f): abundance, supply; (pl.) forces, troops, wealth

coram (adv.): in person, openly

corpus, -oris (n): body

cotidianus, -a, -um: daily

creber, -bra, -brum: dense, crowded, frequent

culpa, -ae (f): blame

cum (conj.): when, since, although

cum . . . tum . . : both . . . and . . .

cum (prep. w. abl.): with

cunctor, -ari, -atus sum: to hesitate, delay

cupide, -ius, -issime (adv.): eagerly

curo, -are, -avi, -atum (with acc. and gerund): to see to, cause to be done

currus, -us (m): chariot

cursus, -us (m): speed, course

de (prep. w. abl.): down from, concerning, about

decimus, -a, -um: tenth

declivis, -e: sloping down

dedecus, -oris (n): a disgrace

deditio, -onis (f): surrender

dedo, -ere, dedidi, deditum: to give up, surrender

deduco, -ere, -duxi, -ductum: to lead down, conduct, bring

defatigo, -are, -avi, -atum: to wear out, exhaust

defectio, -onis (f): rebellion, revolt

defendo, -ere, -di, -sum: to defend, protect

defero, -ferre, -tuli, -latum: to carry down, report

deficio, -ere, -feci, -fectum: to revolt, fail, be wanting

defigo, -ere, -fixi, -fixum: to fasten down, fix

deicio, -icere, -ieci, -iectum: to throw down

deinceps (adv.): in turn, in succession

deinde (adv.): next, then

(94)

deligo, -are, -avi, -atum: to tie, moor
deligo, -ere, -legi, -lectum: to choose, pick out
delitesco, -ere, -litui: to lie hid, lurk
demeto, -ere, -messui, -messum: to cut off, gather, harvest
demonstro, -are, -avi, -atum: to point out, mention, show
deni, -ae, -a: ten each, ten
denique (adv.): finally
depereo, -ire, -ii: to perish, be lost
depono, -ere, -posui, -positum: to lay aside, down, lose
desidero, -are, -avi, -atum: to long for, desire, miss
desilio, -ire, -silui, -sultum: to jump down
desisto, -ere, -stiti, -stitum: to cease
desum, -esse, -fui: to be wanting; (w. dat.) to fail, desert
detrimentum, -i (n): loss, damage, ruin
dico, -ere, dixi, dictum: to say, name, mention, speak
dies, -ei (m. and f.): day
differo, -ferre, distuli, dilatum: to postpone, delay
difficultas, -atis (f): difficulty
dimico, -are, -avi, -atum: to fight, struggle, contend
dimidium, -i (n): half
dimitto, -ere, -misi, -missum: to send about, dismiss, release
discedo, -ere, -cessi, -cessum: to withdraw, depart, go away
dispar, -is: unequal
dispergo, -ere, -spersi, -um: to disperse, scatter
dispono, -ere, -posui, -positum: to arrange, station at different
   points
distribuo, -ere, -ui, -utum: to distribute, assign
diu, diutius, diutissime (adv.): for a long time
divido, -ere, -visi, -visum: to separate, divide
do, dare, dedi, datum: to give
domesticus, -a, -um: internal, at home, civil (of war)
domus, -us or **-i** (f) house, home; **domum:** homewards; **domi:**
   at home; **domo:** from home
ducenti, -ae, -a: two hundred
duco, -ere, duxi, ductum: to lead, consider
dum (conj.): while, until
duo, -ae, -o: two
duodeni, -ae, -a: twelve each, twelve
duplico, -are, -avi, -atum: to double
dux, -cis (c): leader, chief, guide

e, ex (prep. w. abl.)**:** out of, from
efficio, -ere, -feci, -fectum: to accomplish, do
effugio, -ere, -fugi, -fugitum: to escape
ego: I
egredior, -gredi, -gressus sum: to go out, disembark
egregius, -a, -um: eminent, outstanding, excellent
egregie (adv.)**:** excellently, exceedingly, very well
egressus, -us (m)**:** a going out, departure, landing
eicio, -ere, eieci, eiectum: to throw out; **se eicio**—to rush out
emitto, -ere, -misi, -missum: to send out
enim (conj.)**:** for
eo (adv.)**:** to that place; **eo . . . quod . . . :** on his account . . . because
eques, -itis (m)**:** horseman, rider; (pl.) cavalry
equester, -tris, -tre: on horseback, of cavalry
equitatus, -us (m)**:** cavalry
equus, -i (m)**:** horse
eruptio, -onis (f)**:** sally, sortie
essedarius, -i (m)**:** charioteer
essedum, -i (n)**:** chariot
et (conj.)**:** and, also
etiam (conj.)**:** also, even
etsi (conj.)**:** although, even if
evenio, -ire, -veni, -ventum: to result, turn out
eventus, -us (m)**:** outcome, result
examino, -are, -avi, -atum: to weigh
excedo, -ere, -cessi, -cessum: to go away, out, to leave
excipio, -ere, -cepi, -ceptum: to support, relieve, meet
excludo, -ere, -si, -sum: to cut off, hinder, prevent
excuso, -are, -avi, -atum: to excuse, (w. se) to apologize for
exeo, -ire, -ii, -itum: to go out
exercitatio, -onis (f)**:** training, practice
exercitus, -us (m)**:** army
exiguitas, -atis (f)**:** smallness, fewness
exiguus, -a, -um: small, scanty
existimo, -are, -avi, -atum: to think, consider, believe
expeditio, -onis (f)**:** raid, expedition
expeditus, -a, -um: unimpeded, light-armed, free
expello, -ere, -puli, -pulsum: to drive out
exploro, -are, -avi, -atum: to spy out, reconnoitre, seek
expono, -ere, -posui, -positum: to expose, explain, land

exspecto, -are, -avi, -atum: to wait for
exsto, -are, -stiti: to stand out, above
extraho, -ere, -traxi, -tractum: to spin out, protract
extremus, -a, -um: most distant, last, rear, at the back

faber, -bri (m): smith, carpenter, workman
facilis, -e: easy
facio, -ere, feci, factum: to do, make
facultas, -atis (f): chance, opportunity
fagus, -i (f): beech-tree
fas (indecl. n.): right
feliciter (adv.): well, successfully, fortunately
fere (adv.): almost, generally
fero, ferre, -tuli, -latum: to carry, bring, endure
ferreus, -a, -um: iron, of iron
fidelis, -e: faithful, trustworthy, loyal
fides, -ei (f): faith, loyalty
figura, -ae (f): figure, shape, form
finis, -is (m): end; (pl.) boundaries, territory, land
fio, fieri, factus sum: to become, be done
firmiter (adv.): firmly
firmus, -a, -um: strong, firm, stable
flecto, -ere, -xi, -xum: to turn, bend, turn round
fluctus, -us (m): wave
flumen, -inis (n): river
fortis, -e: strong, brave
fortiter, -ius, -issime: bravely
fortuna, -ae (f): fortune, good or bad luck
fossa, -ae (f): ditch, trench
frater, -tris (m): brother
frigus, -oris (n): cold
frumentarius, -a, -um: belonging to corn; **res frumentaria:**
  corn supply
frumentum, -i (n): corn, grain; (pl.) crops
frustra (adv.): in vain
fuga, -ae (f): flight, escape; **in fugam dare:** to put to flight
fugio, -ere, fugi, -itum: to flee, escape, avoid
funda, -ae (f): sling
funis, -is (m): rope, cable

Gallia, -ae (f): Gaul

(97)

Gallicus, -a, -um: Gallic
gallina, -ae (f): hen, fowl
gens, gentis (f): tribe
genus, -eris (n): kind, sort, family
gero, -ere, gessi, gestum: to carry on, do, manage, wage
gladius, -i (m): sword
gravis, -e: heavy, serious, severe
gravitas, -atis (f): weight, severity, importance
gubernator, -oris (m): helmsman
gusto, -are, -avi, -atum: to taste

habeo, -ere, -ui, -itum: to have, hold, consider
hiberna, -orum (n. pl.): winter quarters
hic, haec, hoc: this
hiemo, -are, -avi, -atum: to winter
hiems, -iemis (f): winter, storm, bad weather
homo, -inis (m): man, human being
hora, -ae (f): hour
horridus, -a, -um: wild, rough, savage
hortor, -ari, -atus sum: to urge, encourage, cheer
hostis, -is (m): enemy
huc (adv.): hither, to this place
humanus, -a, -um: civilized

iacio, -ere, ieci, iactum: to throw
iam (adv.): now, already
ibi (adv.): there
idem, eadem, idem: same
idoneus, -a, -um: suitable, capable, convenient
ignoro, -are, -avi, -atum: to be ignorant of, not to know
ignosco, -ere, -novi, -notum: (w. dat.) to pardon, forgive
ignotus, -a, -um: unknown
ille, -a, -ud: that, he, she, it
illo (adv.): thither, to that place
impedio, -ire, -ivi, -itum: to hamper, hinder, obstruct
impeditus, -a, -um: encumbered, preoccupied
imperator, -oris (m): general, commander-in-chief
imperitus, -a, -um: inexperienced, unacquainted with
imperium, -i (n): command, authority
impero, -are, -avi, -atum: (w. dat.) to order, command
impetro, -are, -avi, -atum: to get, obtain

(98)

impetus, -us (m): attack
importo, -are, -avi, -atum: to import, bring in
improvisus, -a, -um: unforeseen
imprudens, -entis: unwise, off one's guard
imprudentia, -ae (f): ignorance, lack of foresight
in (prep. w. acc.): to, towards, into, against
incendium, -i (n): fire
incendo, -ere, -di, -sum: to set fire to, kindle
incertus, -a, -um: uncertain, vague
incipio, -ere, -cepi, -ceptum: to begin
incito, -are, -avi, atum: to urge on, excite, raise up
incognitus, -a, -um: unknown
incolo, -ere, -colui, -cultum: to inhabit, dwell
incolumis, -e: safe
incommodum, -i (n): disaster, disadvantage
incursio, -onis (f): raid, attack
inde (adv.): thence, then
ineo, -ire, -ii, -itum: to enter, begin
inferior, -ius (comp. adj.): lower
infero, -ferre, -tuli, -latum: to bring to (**bellum inferre**—to wage war)
inficio, -ere, -feci, -fectum: to stain, dye
infinitus, -a, -um: boundless, unlimited
infirmus, -a, -um: weak
infra (adv.): below
ingens, -ntis: great, huge, immense
iniquus, -a, -um: unequal, unfavourable
initium, -i (n): beginning
iniuria, -ae (f): wrong, injustice
inquam: I say
insequor, -i, -secutus sum: to follow close, pursue
insinuo, -are, -avi, -atum: to penetrate, to work one's way into
insisto, -ere, -stiti: to stand on
instabilis, -e: unsteady, unstable
instituo, -ere, -ui, -utum: to arrange, begin, resolve
institutum, -i (n): custom, practice, arrangement
instruo, -ere, -struxi, -structum: to draw up, equip
insuefactus, -a, -um: accustomed
insula, -ae (f): island
integer, -gra, -grum: fresh, unharmed, perfect
intellego, -ere, -exi, -ectum: to learn, know, perceive

(99)

inter (prep. w. acc.): among, between
intercedo, -ere, -cessi, -cessum: to pass between, intervene, occur
intercludo, -ere, -clusi, -clusum: to cut off, block
interdico, -ere, -dixi, -dictum: to forbid, prohibit
interea (adv.): meanwhile
interficio, -ere, -feci, -fectum: to kill
interim (adv.): meanwhile
interior, -ius (comp. adj.): inside, inner
intermitto, -ere, -misi, -missum: to let pass, leave a gap, elapse
intervallum, -i (n): interval
introitus, -us (m): entrance
inusitatus, -a, -um: unusual, extraordinary
inutilis, -e: useless
invenio, -ire, -veni, -ventum: to find, learn
ipse, -a, -um: self, very
is, ea, id: that, this, he, she, it
ita (adv.): so, thus
itaque (conj.): and so, therefore
item (adv.): besides
iter, itineris (n): journey, march
iubeo, -ēre, iussi, iussum: to order
iudico, -are, -avi, -atum: to judge, decide
iugum, -i (n): yoke, ridge
ius, iuris (n): right, duty

Labienus, -i (m): legate of Caesar
labor, -oris (m): work, toil, exertion
laboro, -are, -avi, -atum: to toil, be hard pressed
labrum, -i (n): lip
lac, lactis (n): milk
lacesso, -ere, -ivi, -itum: to harass, provoke, challenge
latus, -eris (n): side, flank
latus, -a, -um: wide, broad
laudo, -are, -avi, -atum: to praise
legatio, -onis (f): embassy
legatus, -i (m): envoy, lieutenant
legio, -onis(f): legion
lenis, -e: gentle, mild
lepus, -oris (m): hare
lex, legis (f): law

liberaliter (adv.): graciously, courteously
liberi, -orum (m. pl.): children
libero, -are, -avi, -atum: to set free, release
litus, -oris (n): shore
locus, -i (m): place
longe, -ius, -issime (adv.): far, far off
longinquus, -a, -um: far removed, distant
longus, -a, -um: long
loquor, -i, locutus sum: to speak
Lugotrix, -igis (m): a British chieftain
luna, -ae (f): moon
lux, lucis (f): light, dawn

magnitudo, -inis (f): size
magnopere, magis, maxime (adv.): greatly
magnus, -a, -um: great, important
mandatum, -i (n): order, comand
mando, -are, -avi, -atum: to order, instruct
Mandubracius, -i (m): son of a king of the Trinobantes
mane (adv.): in the morning
maneo, -ēre, mansi, mansum: to remain
manus, -us (f): hand, body of troops
mare, -is (n): the sea
maritimus, -a, -um: belonging to the sea, maritime
materia, -ae (f): timber
maturus, -a, -um: ripe
mediterraneus, -a, -um: inland
medius, -a, -um: middle
membrum, -i (n): limb
mensura, -ae (f): measurement
mercator, -oris (m): trader, merchant
meridianus, -a, -um: of midday
meridies, -ei (m): midday
meto, -ere, messui, messum: to reap
meus, -a, -um: my, mine
miles, militis (m): soldier
militaris, -e: military
mille: a thousand
minime (superl. adv.): by no means, least
minor, minus (comp. adj.): less
mitto, -ere, misi, missum: to send, throw

(101)

mobilitas, -atis (f): speed, quickness
moderor, -ari, -atus sum: to check, control
modo (adv.): merely, only
modus, -i (m): manner, way, kind
mollis, -e: soft
moneo, -ēre, -ui, -itum: to warn, advise
mons, -ntis (m): mountain
Morini, -orum (m. pl.): a Belgic tribe
moror, -ari, -atus sum: to delay
mors, mortis (f): death
mos, moris (m): custom
motus, -us (m): movement, disturbance, sudden rising
moveo, -ēre, movi, motum: to move
multitudo, -inis (f): multitude, number
multus, -a, -um: much, many
munio, -ire, -ivi, -itum: to fortify
munitio, -onis (f): fortification, rampart

nam (conj.): for
namque (conj.): for indeed
nanciscor, -i, nactus sum: to obtain
nascor, -i, natus sum: to be born
natio, -onis (f): tribe
natura, -ae (f): nature
natus, -i (subst.): child, son
nauta, -ae (m): sailor
navalis, -e: naval
navigatio, -onis (f): sailing, navigation
navigium, -i (n): vessel
navigo, -are, -avi, -atum: to sail
navis, -is (f): ship
ne: not
nec: see **neque**
necessarius, -a, -um: necessary
necesse (indecl. adj.): necessary
negotium, -i (n): business, employment, difficulty
nemo: no one, nobody
nequaquam (adv.): by no means
neque or nec: nor, and not
nihil (indecl. n.): nothing, not
nisi (conj.): unless, except

(102)

nobilis, -e: noble, of high birth
noceo, -ēre, -ui, -itum (w. dat.): to hurt, injure
noctu (adv.): by night
nocturnus, -a, -um: in the night
nolo, nolle, nolui: to be unwilling
nominatim (adv.): by name
non: not
nondum (adv.): not yet
nonus, -a, -um: ninth
nos: we
noster, -tra, -trum: our
notus, -a, -um: known, well known
novus, -a, -um: new
nox, noctis (f): night
nullus, -a, -um: no, none
numerus, -i (m): number
nummus, -i (m): coin
numquam (adv.): never
nunc (adv.): now
nuntio, -are, -avi, -atum: to announce
nuntius, -ii (m): messenger, news
nutus, -us (m): nod

ob (prep. w. acc.): on account of, for, towards
obicio, -ere, -ieci, -iectum: to throw in the way, oppose
obses, -sidis (c): hostage, surety
obtempero, -are, -avi, -atum (w. dat.): to submit to, obey
obtineo, -ēre, -ui, -tentum: to hold, possess, preserve
occasio, -onis (f): opportunity
occasus, -us (m): setting, the west
occidens, -entis (m): the West
occido, -ere, -cidi, -cisum: to strike down, kill, slay
occulto, -are, -avi, -atum: to hide, conceal
occupatio, -onis (f): business, affairs
occupo, -are, -avi, -atum: to seize, occupy
occurro, -ere, -curri, -cursum (w. dat.): to meet, attack
Oceanus, -i (m): ocean, sea
octo: eight
oculus, -i (m): eye
officium, -i (n): favour, duty, service
omnino (adv.): entirely, at all

(103)

omnis, -e: all, every
onerarius, -a, -um: transport
onus, -eris (n): weight, cargo
opera, -ae (f): work, care, attention
opinio, -onis (f): belief, opinion, expectation
oportet (impers.): it is necessary, proper
oppidum, -i (n): town
opportune (adv.): opportunely
opportunus, -a, -um: convenient, suitable
opprimo, -ere, -essi, -essum: to overwhelm, crush, press against
oppugno, -are, -avi, -atum: to attack, assail
optimus, -a, -um: best
opus, -eris (n): work, labour
ora, -ae (f): border, edge, coast
orator, -oris (m): speaker, ambassador
ordo, -inis (m): rank, line, series
orior, -iri, ortus sum: to rise, appear
ostendo, -ere, -di, -sum or -tum: to show, display, declare

pabulator, -oris (m): forager
pabulor, -ari, -atus sum: to forage, seek food
pagus, -i (m): district, region
palus, -udis (f): marsh, swamp
par, paris: equal
parens, parentis (c): parent, father or mother
paro, -are, -avi, -atum: to prepare
pars, partis (f): part, side
passus, -us (m): step, pace (**mille passus** = mile)
pater, -tris (m): father
patior, -i, passus sum: to endure, suffer, allow
paucitas, -atis (f): fewness, scarcity
paucus, -a, -um: few, little
paulatim (adv.): little by little, gradually
paulisper (adv.): for a little while, for a short time
paulo/paulum (adv.): a little, somewhat
pax, pacis (f): peace
pecus, -oris (n): cattle, herd, flock
pedes, -itis (m): infantryman
pedester, -tris, -tre: on foot
peditatus, -us (m): infantry

pellis, -is (f): skin, hide
pendo, -ere, pependi, pensum: to weigh, pay
per (prep. w. acc.): through, by means of
percontatio, -onis (f): question, inquiry
percurro, -ere, -cucurri, -cursum: to run along
perduco, -ere, -duxi, -ductum: to lead through, win over
perequito, -are, -avi, -atum: to drive through
perexiguus, -a, -um: very small, very little
perfero, -ferre, -tuli, -latum: to carry through, arrive
perfuga, -ae (m): deserter
periculum, -i (n): danger
permaneo, -ēre, -mansi, -mansum: to remain, continue
permitto, -ere, -misi, -missum: to entrust, surrender, allow
permoveo, -ēre, -movi, motum: to influence, excite, alarm
perpaucus, -a, -um: very little, very few
perpetuus, -a, -um: continuous, unbroken
perrumpo, -ere, -rupi, -ruptum: to break through, overcome
persequor, -i, -secutus sum: to follow after, pursue
perspicio, -ere, -spexi, -spectum: to look at, explore, inspect
perterreo, -ēre, -ui, -itum: to thoroughly frighten
pertineo, -ēre, -ui: to reach, extend, affect
perturbatio, -onis (f): disturbance, confusion
perturbo, -are, -avi, -atum: confuse, disturb
pervenio, -ire, -veni, -ventum (w. ad + acc.) to reach, arrive at
pes, pedis (m): foot
peto, -ere, -ivi, -itum: to seek, attack, make for
planus, -a, -um: level, flat, even
plenus, -a, -um: full
plerumque (adv.): for the most part, mostly, usually
plerique, pleraeque, pleraque: most
plumbum, -i (n): lead; **plumbum album**—tin
plus, -ris (comp. adj.): more
polliceor, -ēri, -itus sum: promise, offer
pondus, -eris (n): weight
populus, -i (m): people, nation
porta, -ae (f): gate
porto, -are, -avi, -atum: to carry
portus, -us (m): harbour
possum, posse, potui: to be able, have influence
post (prep. w. acc.): behind, after
postea (adv.): afterwards

(105)

posterus, -a, -um: next, coming after
postridie (adv.): on the next day
postulo, -are, -avi, -atum: to demand, ask, request
praeceps, -cipitis: headlong, steep
praecludo, -ere, -si, -sum: to shut up, close, hinder
praeda, -ae (f): booty, plunder
praedico, -are, -avi, -atum: to proclaim, declare
praedor, -ari, -atus sum: to plunder
praeficio, -ere, -feci, -fectum: to put in command
praefigo, -ere, -xi, -xum: to set in front
praemitto, -ere, -misi, -missum: to send in advance, forward
praeparo, -are, -avi, -atum: to prepare beforehand
praesidium, -i (n): protection, garrison
praesto, -are, -stiti, -stitum: to fulfil
praesum, -esse, -fui: to be in command over
praeter (prep. w. acc.): beyond
praeterea (adv.): besides
premo, -ere, -ssi, -ssum: to oppress, press hard
pridie (adv.): on the day before
primo (adv.): at first, firstly
primus, -a, -um: first, foremost
primum (adv.): at first, firstly
princeps, -cipis: first; also noun—chief, leading man
prior, -oris (comp. adj.): former
pristinus, -a, -um: previous, original
priusquam (conj.): before
privatus, -a, -um: private
pro (prep. w. abl.): in front of, on account of
probo, -are, -avi, -atum: to try, test, approve of
procedo, -ere, -cessi, -cessum: to advance, show one's self
prodo, -ere, -didi, -ditum: to bring forward, surrender, betray
produco, -ere, -duxi, -ductum: to lead forward, draw out
proelior, -ari, -atus sum: to join battle, fight
proelium, -i (n): battle
proficiscor, -i, profectus sum: to set out
progredior, -i, progressus sum: to advance
prohibeo, -ēre, -ui, -itum: to hold back, check, prevent
proicio, -ere, -ieci, -iectum: to throw forward, drive, expel
promissus: hanging down, long
prope (prep. w. acc.): near; (adv.): nearly
propello, -ere, -puli, -pulsum: to drive, propel

(106)

propinquus, -a, -um: near, neighbouring
propter (prep. w. acc.): on account of, owing to, because of
propugno, -are, -avi, -atum: to go out to fight, fight in defence of
prosequor, -i, -secutus sum: to follow, pursue
prospectus, -us (m): look out, distant view
protinus (adv.): straightway, continuously
proveho, -ere, -xi, -ectum: to carry forward, convey, transport
provideo, -ēre, -vidi, -visum: to foresee, provide for
proximus, -a, -um: nearest, next
pugna, -ae (f): fight, combat ‑
pugno, -are, -avi, -atum: to fight, engage in battle
pulvis, -eris (m): dust
puto, -are, -avi, -atum: to think, believe, consider

quaestor, -oris (m): quaestor, treasurer
quam (adv.): how, as, than; + superl. = as . . . as possible
quantus, -a, -um: how great, as much as
quartus, -a, -um: fourth
quattuor: four
queror, -i, questus sum: to complain, lament
qui, quae, quod: who, which
quicumque: whoever, whatever
quinque: five
quintus, -a, -um: fifth
quisquam, quaequam, quicquam (indef. pron.): anyone, anything
quisque, quaeque, quodque (indef. pron.): each
quo (adv.): whither
quoad (adv.): how long
quod (conj.): because
quoniam (conj.): since
quoque (conj.): also
quum (conj.): when, since

rado, -ere, rasi, rasum: to shave
rarus, -a, -um: here and there
ratio, -onis (f): account, reckoning, plan, system
rebellio, -onis (f): renewal of war, revolt
recens, -entis: fresh, recent

(107)

recipio, -ere, -cepi, -ceptum: to take back, regain, recover; (w. **se**) to retreat
redeo, -ire, -ii, -itum: to return
reditus, -us (m): return
reduco, -ere, -duxi, -ductum: to lead back, withdraw
refero, -ferre, -tuli, -latum: to carry, bring back; **pedem referre** = to retreat
reficio, -ere, -feci, -fectum: to restore, rebuild, repair
regio, -onis (f): boundary, country, district
reicio, -ere, -ieci, -iectum: to throw back, repel, force back
relinquo, -ere, -liqui, -lictum: to leave behind, abandon
reliquus, -a, -um: remaining, left.
remaneo, -ēre, -mansi: to stay, remain behind
remigo, -are, -avi, -atum: to row
remigro, -are, -avi, -atum: to journey back, return, retire.
remissior (comp. adj.): mild
remitto, -ere, -misi, -missum: to send back, release, dispatch
removeo, -ēre, -movi, -motum: to move back, remove, set aside
remus, -i (m): oar
renuntio, -are, -avi, -atum: to declare, announce, report
repello, -ere, -ppuli, -pulsum: to drive back, repel
repente (adv.): suddenly
repentinus, -a, -um: sudden, unlooked for, unexpected
reperio, -ire, -pperi, -pertum: to find, discover
reporto, -are, -avi, -atum: to carry, bring back
res, rei (f): consult a dictionary for the meaning of this word
respublica, reipublicae (f): the state, republic
revertor, -i, reversus sum: to turn back, return
revoco, -are, -avi, -atum: to recall, command to return
rex, regis (m): king
ripa, -ae (f): river-bank
rota, -ae (f): wheel
Rufus, -i (m): Publius Sulpicius Rufus, one of Caesar's officers
rursus (adv.): back again, again

Sabinus, -i (m): one of Caesar's legati
saepe (adv.): often
sagitta, -ae (f): arrow
satis (adv.): enough, sufficient
scapha, -ae (f): light boat, skiff
scribo, -ere, -psi, -ptum: to write, draw

(108)

se: himself, herself, itself
secundus, -a, -um: following, second
sed (conj.): but
Segonax, -acis (m): one of the four kings of Kent
Segontiaci, -orum (m. pl.): a small British tribe
semita, -ae (f): path
sententia, -ae (f): opinion, judgement
septem: seven
septentrio, -onis (m): the north, seven plough stars
septimus, -a, -um: seventh
sequor, -i, secutus sum: seventh
sero, -ere, sevi, satum: to sow, plant
servo, -are, -avi, -atum: to keep, preserve, protect
si (conj.): if
sic (adv.): so, thus
signum, -i (n): signal, standard
silva, -ae (f): wood
silvestris, -e: wooded, woody
simul (adv.): at the same time
sine (prep. w. abl.): without
singularis, -e: single, alone, one by one
singuli, -ae, -a (distrib. adj.): one apiece, one each
sinister, -tra, -trum: left, unfavourable
sol, solis (m): sun
solus, -a, -um: alone, only
solvo, -ere, solvi, solutum: to loosen, disengage, set sail
spatium, -i (n): space, interval, distance
species, -ei (f): appearance, shape, view
specto, -are, -avi, -atum: to look at, view, gaze at
speculatoria, -ae (f): spy-boat
spes, -ei (f): hope
stabilitas, -atis (f): firmness, stability
statim (adv.): immediately, at once
statio, -onis (f): guard, position, place
statuo, -ere, -ui, -utum: to set up, position, resolve
strepitus, -us (m): noise, din
studium, -i (n): enthusiasm, eagerness, desire
sub (prep. w. acc. or abl.): under, beneath
subduco, -ere, -duxi, -ductum: to draw up, beach, raise
subeo, -ire, -ii, -itum: to go under, approach, advance
subito (adv.): suddenly, unexpectedly

subministro, -are, -avi, -atum: to supply, furnish
submitto, -ere, -misi, -missum: to send up, supply, produce
submoveo, -ēre, -movi, -motum: to dislodge, remove, ward off
subsequor, -i, -secutus sum: to follow close, pursue
subsidium, -i (n): reinforcement, aid
subsisto, -ere, -stiti: to halt, hold
subsum, -esse, -fui: to be near at hand
succedo, -ere, -cessi -cessum: to come after, take place of, enter
succido, -ere, -cidi, -cisum: to cut down, cut through
sudis, -is (f): stake
suffero, -erre, sustuli, sublatum: to carry under, bear, support
summus, -a, -um: highest
superior, -ius (comp. adj.): previous, former, upper
supero, -are, -avi, -atum: to go over, overcome, conquer
supersum, -esse, -fui: to be left over, remain, survive
supra (prep. w. acc.): above
suspicio, -onis (f): suspicion
suspicor, -ari, -atus sum: to mistrust, suspect
sustineo, -ēre, -ui, -tentum: to hold up, support, check
suus, -a, -um: his own, her own, etc.

talea, -ae (f): bar, ingot
tamen (adv.): nevertheless, however, yet
tantulus, -a, -um: so little, so small
tantus, -a, -um: of such size, so great
tardius (comp. adv.): more slowly, somewhat slowly
Taximagulus, -i (m): one of the four kings of Kent
tego, -ere, -xi, -ctum: to cover, hide, conceal
telum, -i (n): weapon, missile
temere (adv.): rashly
temo, -onis (m): beam, pole
tempero, -are, -avi, -atum: to temper, qualify, rule
tempestas, -atis (f): weather, storm
tempus, -oris (n): time, season, occasion
teneo, -ēre, -ui, tentum: to hold, retain, keep, check
tergum, -i (n): the back, rear
terra, -ae (f): land, earth
terror, -oris (m): fear, horror
tertius, -a, -um: third
testudo, -inis (f): tortoise

timor, -oris (m): dread, terror
tormentum, -i (n): engine of war, artillery
tollo, -ere, sustuli, sublatum: to lift up, raise up
tot: so many
totus, -a, -um: whole, entire
traicio, -ere, -ieci, -iectum: to throw across, convey across
tranquillitas, -atis (f): stillness, calm, peacefulness
transeo, -ire, -ii, -itum: to go across, cross over
transmitto, -ere, -misi, -missum: to send across, despatch, transmit
transporto, -are, -avi, -atum: to remove, transport, convey across
tres, tria: three
tribunus, -i (m): tribune
Trinobantes, -um (m. pl.): a tribe of East Anglia
tripertito (adv.): in three parts
triquetrus, -a, -um: triangular, three-cornered
tueor, -ēri, tuitus sum: to defend, protect
turma, -ae (f): troop, squadron

ubi (conj.): where, when
ullus, -a, -um: any, anyone
ulterior, -ius (comp. adj.): further, farther
ultro (adv.): on the further side, beyond what is expected
umquam (adv.): at any time, ever
unde (adv.): whence
undique (adv.): from all sides, from everywhere
universus, -a, -um: all together, whole
unus, -a, -um: one, single
usus, -us (m): use, experience, practice
ut(i) (adv. and conj.): as, that, so that
uter, utra, utrum (pron.): which of two
uterque, -traque, -trumque: both, both sides
utor, -i, usus sum: to use, enjoy
uxor, -oris (f): wife

vadum, -i (n): ford, shoal
vagor, -ari, -atus sum: to wander, roam, range
vallum, -i (n): rampart, wall
vasto, -are, -avi, -atum: to desert, lay waste
vectigal, -alis (n): tax, tribute

(III)

vectorius, -a, -um: for transport
Veneticus, -a, -um: belonging to the Veneti
venio, -ire, veni, ventum: to come
ventito, -are, -avi, -atum: to keep coming, come often
ventus, -i (m): wind
verbum, -i (n): word
vereor, -ēri, -itus sum: to fear, be afraid, revere
vergo, -ere: to turn, incline, bend
vero (adv.): indeed, moreover
vestio, -ire, -ivi, -itum: to clothe
veto, -are, -ui, -itum: to forbid, prohibit
via, -ae (f): road
vicies (adv.): twenty times
video, -ere, vidi, visum: to see
vigilia, -ae (f): watch
vinculum -i (n): chain, bond
virgo, -inis (f): maiden
virtus, -utis (f): bravery, courage, valour
vis, vim, vi (f): force, violence; in pl. strength
vito, -are, -avi, -atum: to avoid, shun
vitrum, -i (n): woad
vivo, -ere, -ixi, -ictum: to live
vix (adv.): scarcely
voco, -are, -avi, -atum: to call, summon, invoke
volo, velle, volui: to wish, desire, want
voluptas, -atis (f): satisfaction, delight, pleasure
Volusenus, -i (m): a tribune in Caesar's army
vox, vocis (f): voice
vulgo (adv.): generally
vulnus, -eris (n): wound
vultus, -us (m): expression, features, face